TESTIFYING IN COURT

Second Edition

TESTIFYING IN COURT

A guide for physicians

Jack E. Horsley, J.D.
With John Carlova

Medical Economics Books
Oradell, New Jersey 07649

Library of Congress Cataloging in Publication Data

Horsley, Jack E.
Testifying in court.

Includes index.
1. Medical jurisprudence—United States. 2. Evidence, Expert—United States. I. Carlova, John. II. Title.
[DNLM: 1. Expert testimony. W 725 H818t]
KF8964.Z9H65 1983 347.73'67 83-863
ISBN 0-87489-315-1 347.30767

Cover design by Douglas Steel

ISBN 0-87489-315-1

Medical Economics Company Inc.
Oradell, New Jersey 07649

First Edition 1972
Second Printing 1975
Second Edition 1983

Printed in the United States of America

CONTENTS

FOREWORD

Sooner or later, most practicing physicians will testify in court. Basically, these appearances fall into three categories: (1) the "fact" witness, who's usually called to testify about the condition of a patient he's examined or treated; (2) the "opinion" or expert witness, who tries to help the judge and jury reach conclusions on medical issues; and, most important, (3) the doctor-defendant in a malpractice suit, whose career may depend on the effectiveness of his testimony.

Too often, however, doctors succumb to what I call "court fright." This is more virulent than "stage fright," and it strikes with surprising frequency. In 50 years as a trial lawyer, I've seen it undercut the effectiveness of witnesses who normally were persons with poise, intelligence, and strength of character.

Just one example: I represented the plaintiff in a medical malpractice case, during which a prominent surgeon was called by the defense as an expert witness. As he came through the courtroom doorway, he seemed a formidable fellow—tall and distinguished-looking, with an authoritative manner.

When he began that long walk to the witness stand, though, he looked as though he were approaching the electric chair. Almost literally, he went to pieces with "court fright." His knees seemed to buckle, and he glanced wildly about the courtroom, as though seeking escape. He was so flustered, he even tried to shake the hand of the court clerk, who was waiting to swear him in.

The watching jurors couldn't help but wonder, "Why is this witness so panicky and frightened?" He had one strike on him before he even took the stand.

On the stand, he alternated between fidgeting and slumping in the seat, with one hand restlessly wandering over his face. At one point during his testimony, he grinned at someone in the spectators' section. Later, he scowled fiercely at me as I started my cross-examination. Two strikes on him.

There was no doubt that this doctor was an expert in his field. The trouble was that he devalued his own testimony by the way he presented it. He went on and on about his credentials until they became boring to the jurors. In answering my questions, he was hostile and evasive, which created the impression that he was hiding something.

Then he committed the cardinal sin of a witness—he lost his temper. He fumed and growled at me as he responded grudgingly to my questions.

Strike three. Despite his medical expertise, that doctor was a loser as a witness.

Compare his performance with that of a cardiologist who testified in another case I tried.

He approached the stand in a normal manner, glancing to neither right nor left, using the waiting court clerk as a focal point. On the stand, he sat upright, with his feet firmly on the floor, his hands resting in a comfortable position, his attention concentrated on the lawyer questioning him. He responded concisely, to the point, and with refreshing candor. If he didn't know an answer, he said so.

When he used medical terms, he sometimes explained them, but not to the extent of talking down to jurors. He addressed them as he would a patient—not as a lecturer, but as a teacher imparting his medical knowledge and giving advice and guidance.

Despite his low-key manner, he came through as a compassionate, caring person—realistic and objective in his views. In short, he was a good doctor who had brought his bedside manner with him to court; and it worked. He was a winner.

How can you be a winner on the witness stand? How can you overcome "court fright"? How should you prepare for an appearance on the stand? What fee should you charge—if any? How should you handle yourself on direct examination? What's the best way to deal with a tough cross-examiner? What are the booby traps you should avoid?

All those and many more questions are answered in this book.

By reputation, I have known the author, Jack E. Horsley, for many years. He's one of the best medical malpractice defense attorneys in the country. If anyone can prepare a doctor for the witness stand, Jack can. Read his book. It's a winner.

Melvin M. Belli Sr.
San Francisco

PUBLISHER'S NOTES

Jack E. Horsley, J.D., is a specialist in medico-legal matters who has been practicing law for more than 40 years. He is a Fellow of the American College of Trial Lawyers, a former director of the Society of Trial Lawyers, and Past President of the Illinois Defense Counsel Association. He is a consultant and contributor to *Medical Economics* magazine, and has written extensively on legal subjects. His writings include a text, *Illinois Civil Practice & Procedure,* and numerous treatises and monographs published by the Illinois Continuing Legal Education Institute, Chicago; The Court Practice Institute of Chicago; and The Practicing Law Institute of New York. With John Carlova, he also wrote, *Your Family and the Law,* a book addressed specifically to physicians.

John Carlova, West Coast Editor of *Medical Economics* magazine, is the author or co-author of 12 books. His writings have appeared in *The Reader's Digest, Harper's Magazine, American Heritage, Cosmopolitan, The National Geographic,* and many other leading publications. He has also written for radio, television, and motion pictures.

I

EXPLODING THE MYTHS

Testifying = Terrifying.

Those two words are synonymous to many doctors who appear in court as witnesses. After a recent trial in the Midwest, for example, I spoke to an internist who had just testified. Although he'd appeared in quite a few previous cases as a medical witness, he showed signs of strain.

"I get nervous every time I testify," he told me. "I feel as though I'm all alone up there in that damned witness chair, facing a sea of hostile faces. It seems like everybody in the courtroom is against me."

That same day, I encountered a young surgeon who was making his first appearance in court as a medical witness, and he didn't like the idea one bit. "Now I know what a patient going into the operating room feels like," he said miserably.

There must be thousands of physicians who can identify with one or the other of those two doctors. Whether they're old-timers or newcomers in the witness chair, they have trouble in adjusting to what they feel is the alien, antagonistic atmosphere of the courtroom. The problem may be simple nervousness, or it may be apprehension—but almost always, I've found there's no good reason for it to exist. It's based mainly on myths.

One purpose of this book is to explode those myths. We'll also cover such important items as how to prepare for a court appearance, how to give better depositions in less time, how to determine your witness fee, how to ward off stage fright on the witness stand, how to win over the judge and influence the jury, how to make the most of direct examination, how to use your records to the best advantage as a witness, how to star at presenting an exhibit or putting on a demonstration, how to dodge a cross-examination trap, how to be sure your testimony does not violate doctor-patient confidentiality, and how to handle the tough or tricky cross-examiner.

In short, the book will include all the big things and many of the little ones that cumulatively make for an effective performance on the witness stand.

Contact with the legal process, of course, has long been a fact of professional life for doctors. Back in the days of the Roman Empire, a physician named Antistius examined the bloody remains of Julius Caesar and later performed superbly on the witness stand. Of the 23 stab wounds inflicted, he testified, only one was mortal—the perforation of the thorax. Today the doctor on the stand is the most important of all expert witnesses. Between 60 and 80 per cent of all contested cases at the trial level require medical evidence.

Consequently, virtually every doctor will be called to testify at some time during his or her career. For orthopedists and many other M.D.s who treat or examine accident victims, a court appearance is a regular occurrence. And in a malpractice case, of course, a doctor's career may depend on the effectiveness of his testimony on the witness stand.

The specter of malpractice has haunted the medical profession much longer than some doctors might suppose. The code of Hammurabi in the early Mesopotamian civilization specified that "if a surgeon should treat a gentleman with a bronze lancet and cause either death or loss of an eye, the surgeon's hand should be cut off, but if he causes the loss of a slave, he need only provide a new slave." While today's penalties for malpractice are somewhat less drastic, they're still worrisome for doctors who have to face them in court.

Actually, our system of trial by combat is unnerving to many who enter the legal arena, including lawyers themselves. Attorney Charles P. Curtis has defined the way we administer justice as "an adversary proceeding—which is to say we set the parties fighting." Rufus Choate, the great American lawyer who was a contemporary of Daniel Webster, freely admitted that he always felt wretched during a trial. He used to grumble that he'd invariably spend two sleepless nights, "One in preparing what I was to say in court, and one in lamenting what I had said."

In light of all this, it's not surprising that some doctor-witnesses get nervous before and after taking the stand. The problem isn't the nervousness; it's the inability to control it. The fact is that, if you can control it, nervousness as a witness is good for you. Listen to what Frederic T. Howard, an eminent attorney, has to say on the subject of jitters in court:

"When one rises to cross-examine or make a plea, he will be nervous indeed—that is, if he's any good. His knees will weaken, and his perspiration will flow copiously, but this very fear or stage fright gives presence and magnetism to the sufferer. If he controls it, this repressed emotion is transmitted to his hearers like the effect of a galvanic battery. It gives the idea of great reserved power."

Although those remarks were addressed to young lawyers, they apply equally well to the medical witness. Nervousness stimulates you, keys you up, makes you sharp and alert. Fine. But how do you control it? The first step is to throw out of your mind the most common myth about testifying—that the doctor on the witness stand is all alone and highly vulnerable.

The truth is, the medical witness is in a particularly strong position. First of all, he can expect help from the attorney for his side, who'll be ready to object if the opposing lawyer tries any unfair tactics. The judge will be watching, too—and courts are much more interested in protecting the rights of the witness than you may think. Then there's the jury, those 12 good men (and/or women) and true. They tend to identify more with the witness than with the cross-examiner—*unless* the witness gives them reason to do otherwise.

In sum, everybody is with the witness except the opposing lawyer—and he's not always the formidable fellow he might seem to be. Even if he's studied the medical aspects of the case, he's still a tyro in *your* element. You have the advantage of knowing far more than he does about medicine. Very literally, you're the doctor.

Another myth that creates tension for the medical witness is that doctors and lawyers are natural enemies, like cats and dogs. The physician who goes to court with that attitude is likely to be suspicious, skeptical, or outright belligerent. He's inclined to agree with Dickens's Mr. Bumble, who denounced the law as "a ass—a idiot!" Alas, he may even agree with the British peer who defined a lawyer as "a legal chap who rescues your estate from your enemies and keeps it for himself."

Now, I'm not going to pretend that all lawyers are perfect little gentlemen; we all know better than that. I just want to point out two things: (1) The suspicious, skeptical, or belligerent medical witness usually hurts himself and his side because his testimony tends to be sardonic or truculent—two attributes that juries find distasteful. (2) Most cross-examiners regard the competent medical witness with respect and some trepidation. A veteran attorney, Irving Goldstein, once put it this way:

"The more experience one has in the cross-examination of the medical witness, and particularly the expert medical witness, the more one must come to the conclusion that the cross-examination of a truthful, honest, efficient, and capable expert medical witness who isn't given to exaggeration is not only dangerous but usually harmful to the trial lawyer. When this type of medical witness is encountered, it's no wonder that the most experienced and most successful trial lawyers in personal injury cases frequently feel that the best cross-examination is no cross-examination."

In brief, it's the inept, unprepared, unprepossessing, or unthinking medical witness that the cross-examiner is likely to go for. An insecure doctor on the stand, for example, may try to make himself look good and feel better by puffing up his qualifications. I remember one case in which the medical witness, a G.P., testified that he had surgical privileges at three hospitals. On cross-examination, he was asked whether he actually did any surgery at those hospitals. The answer was "No." Then he was asked if he ever did surgery at all, except for minor office procedures. Again the answer was "No." That doctor's testimony was largely discredited because the jury's attitude was, "This fellow isn't exactly a liar, but he sure doesn't tell the whole truth and nothing but the truth."

This doesn't mean that a G.P., or any other M.D., can't qualify as an expert medical witness. The courts have consistently held that anyone with an M.D. degree may be considered a medical expert, even though he might not be a specialist in the particular ailment that is the subject of the inquiry.

Obviously there is a danger here—the possibility that a doctor may overestimate himself as an expert—and it's one into which more than a few physicians have blundered. Early in a fracture case a few years ago, an elderly G.P.'s expertise was put to a test on the witness stand. He was handed a bone by the cross-examiner and asked to identify the part of the body it came from. After studying the bone, the doctor said it came from a woman's leg. The cross-examiner then revealed that the bone the G.P. was holding had come from a dog. That doctor might just as well have gone home right then and there, for all the influence the rest of his testimony had.

Incidents such as that have built up another courtroom myth: Most cross-examiners are slyly murderous. That one goes back to the days when many trial lawyers were indeed cunning, ruthless, and relentless. During one trial, a witness became so irate when the cross-examiner kept wagging a finger under his nose that he bit the finger. At another trial, a country doctor spit tobacco juice into the eye of a cross-examiner who was badgering him by shaking a book in his face. The lawyer then literally threw the book at the doctor—appropriately, it was Gray's Anatomy. Another attorney of that colorful era once ended a powerful argument with a tear-choked version of "Home, Sweet Home" because his client, a mother of eight, was confined to a hospital.

No trial lawyer today could get away with that. The lugubrious lawyer, like the bullying barrister, is largely a thing of the past. Judges are too intent on maintaining decorum in court, and juries are too sophisticated to be taken in by a corny act. Trial lawyers themselves tend to be low-key. Many even remain seated at the counsel table during cross-examination, rather than closing in on the witness to wag a finger or shake a book.

One note of caution: No matter how subdued a lawyer may seem, if the medical witness gives him an opening, that lawyer is almost sure to reach out and figuratively knock the doctor's block off. During a trial in a rural, southern Illinois town, for example, a rather pompous orthopedist was committing one of the cardinal sins of testifying. He kept spouting scientific terms that mean little or nothing to the layman. The jury of farmers and small-business men looked baffled and annoyed. Finally, the cross-examiner, who'd been lounging at the counsel table, drawled: "Just a moment, Doctor. You keep talking about this here tibia. What is that—a country in Africa?"

"Why, no," the orthopedist replied. "It's the shin bone."

"Ah! *That* I understand. I'd certainly appreciate it, Doctor—and I'm sure the jury would appreciate it, too—if you'd translate all them fancy terms for us countryfolk." And the lawyer rolled his eyes at the jury, as much as to say, "See how I got this dude to speak plain English?" He clearly had the jury on his side.

Another sure way for the medical witness to make a fool of himself is to memorize his testimony as though it were a speech. Cross-examiners love to spot this type of witness—and he's not difficult to spot. The parrot-like intonation and the stiff, artificial structure of his sentences give him away. He's not difficult to demolish, either. The skillful cross-examiner simply diverts the witness from his memorized lines by asking unrelated questions. The witness loses his place, so to speak, and begins to flop and flounder, sometimes blanking out completely on the points he's trying to get across. The jury is led to the conclusion that the witness is either weak-minded or a liar.

When I'm preparing a medical witness for a trial, I especially warn him against memorizing any part of his testimony. I advise him to assemble his ideas, not his words, in effective order. The words, I've learned, take care of themselves.

Another bit of advice I pass on to the medical witness is related to still another myth—that the expert in a court case is expected to know it all. The doctor who takes the stand with this impression is asking for trouble. Cross-examiners have a good ear for the overemphatic statement that marks the medical witness who cherishes his authority. Quite often he can be led into deep waters—medical matters that he has no reason to keep fresh in his mind—and left there to thrash about.

In one case I recall, the doctor compounded his error by angrily sputtering at the cross-examiner: "Are you questioning my competence, sir? Are you suggesting I'm a liar?" He himself planted the seed of discredit in the minds of the jurors, and there was no doubt that it had taken root.

In contrast, consider the behavior of a psychiatrist who was testifying in a California case. When the cross-examiner attempted to question him on a detail of anatomy, the psychiatrist frankly admitted he didn't consider himself an expert in that area.

"But, Doctor," the lawyer protested, "you studied anatomy in medical school, didn't you?"

"Yes."

"Then you must be thoroughly familiar with it."

"I *was*."

"Why do you speak in the past tense?"

"Because there are just two types of people who know all about anatomy. One is the professor in medical school, and the other is the student who's just graduated from the course. I am neither."

The jury respected that man for his candor. No matter how expert a doctor may be in his particular field, he's still a human being subject to limitations of knowledge. When he admits he doesn't know it all, he reveals himself as a human being—and so makes the jury feel closer to him. The moral for the medical witness: If you don't know the answer to a question, or even if you're doubtful about the answer, say so. Indulging in guesswork is one sure road to disaster.

It's also disastrous to go to extremes in your attitude toward opposition medical witnesses. Some doctors on the stand get riled and abusive when their opinions are challenged by other doctors. On the other hand, there are medical witnesses who shy away from what they consider to be unseemly courtroom controversy with opposition doctors. The right attitude to adopt is suggested by Cyril H. Wecht, a physician and lawyer, former Coroner, and now Commissioner of Allegheny County (Pittsburgh), Pennsylvania:

"As physicians, we frequently disagree among ourselves at medical staff meetings, and we take it for granted. There's no reason why we can't do that in court. Say the cross-examiner remarks to you: 'Well, Dr. Jones gave an opinion quite different from yours. Are you telling us that Dr. Jones doesn't know what he's talking about?' The correct answer is, 'No, I'm not saying that at all. Dr. Jones is a competent professional man. However, the subject under discussion here is open to different interpretations, and the one I've given is my opinion. Dr. Jones is entitled to his. I just don't happen to agree with him in this case.' "

Occasionally, a lawyer may attempt to take advantage of a conflict in testimony by medical witnesses. One attorney, who was trying to create doubt in the minds of the jurors during a personal injury case, demanded of the physician on the stand, "Why is it, Doctor, that physicians have so much difficulty in agreeing on points of medicine?" The classic answer was, "Probably for the same reason that the U.S. Supreme Court has so much difficulty in agreeing on points of law."

Dr. Wecht points out another courtroom myth—that doctors are compelled to hang around and waste valuable hours or even days when they're called to testify.

"Whenever that happens to a doctor," says Wecht, "it's almost always his own fault. Some lawyers are consid-

I erate about arranging a case to fit the convenience of a medical witness. Most are just too busy rounding up other witnesses and taking care of details. But if the doctor speaks up and says he doesn't want to wait in court, the lawyer will almost invariably make suitable arrangements. One common method is for the two of them to estimate how long it will take the doctor to get to court from his office. Then, with that in mind, the lawyer alerts the doctor by telephoning when the time for testifying is near. If the doctor is from out of town, the lawyer—or even the judge—will sometimes rearrange the sequence of the trial to suit the doctor. The expert medical witness is a kind of dignitary in court. He can often get special consideration if he just asks for it."

He can also get a more effective performance out of himself if he pays attention to one small but highly significant detail. To wit: Sit up straight in the witness chair. Time after time I've seen the value of a medical witness's testimony discounted because of his slouching appearance on the stand. It might seem easier to curve your spine and cross your legs when sitting down, but it's not. This position calls for frequent shifting of the body and the recrossing of the legs. It's also conducive to such nervous mannerisms as stroking the chin, tugging at an earlobe, scratching the head, or moving the hand over the mouth. As a result, the jurors are likely to get the impression that they're dealing with a shifty, nervous fellow.

The remedy is this: Sit so the lowest part of your back is firmly against the back of the witness chair. Place both feet flat on the floor. Clasp your hands lightly and lean forward just a little. This position, I've had many witnesses tell me, helps greatly to alleviate feelings of nervousness.

It also makes the medical witness *look* confident and capable—a look that's important to the jury. A doctor may be the greatest expert in his field, but if he doesn't look and act the part, he's in trouble with the jury. A jury wants what a patient does—a doctor who's competent, confident, considerate, helpful, and honest. In short, a man they can believe in.

Keep that in mind. It's the secret of success for one of the best medical witnesses I've ever known. I once asked him how he was able to perform so well on the witness stand, and I've been passing along the gist of his answer to other medical witnesses ever since: "When I'm on the stand, I think of the jury as a patient. I go into the medical problem involved, and I explain it just as I would to a patient. And I do my best to get across the truth, just as I would to a patient. It's as simple as that."

Simple? Yes, and also highly effective. The medical witness who thinks of jurors as patients finds himself at ease in a familiar role—the doctor-teacher who's helping laymen to understand and cope with a medical problem. The tensions and distractions of the courtroom fall away, and the doctor-patient relationship takes over. The usual result is satisfaction all around. The jury benefits from the doctor's knowledge, and the doctor comes off the stand with a feeling of professional fulfillment.

Of course, if the doctor has gone onto the stand in the wrong frame of mind—or if he's tried to support an ill-considered case—he may come away in disgrace. We'll go into that aspect of testifying in the following chapter.

"DO I HAVE TO GO TO COURT?" II

A small-town doctor I know was once subpoenaed to testify in a personal injury case. This was the first time he'd ever been called as a medical witness—and, like many another doctor, he wasn't too enthusiastic about the idea. Nevertheless, he carefully read the subpoena and noted that he was to appear in court at 9:30 a.m. on a certain day. Right on time, he walked into the courtroom and sat down in back. For 15 minutes, he listened to two lawyers who were wrangling before the judge. Then the doctor glanced at his watch and got up and walked out.

Later, while making hospital rounds, he was called to the phone by an irate lawyer, who demanded to know why the doctor hadn't appeared in court.

"But I did appear," the doctor mildly replied. "Nobody paid any attention to me, so I disappeared."

He was, of course, compelled to reappear.

That doctor was at least willing to meet the law halfway. I've known many other physicians who were reluctant to meet the law at any point. Time after time I've had doctors telephone me after receiving notice to testify in some case or other. Almost invariably, the big question has been: "Do I *have* to go to court?"

The answer comes in two parts:

1. If you're a "fact" witness—that is, if you treated a patient involved in a legal action, or if you have knowledge pertinent to the case—you must appear in court; you can be brought in by subpoena. In general, therefore, if you receive such a subpoena, don't ignore it. Failure to appear can result in a contempt of court citation against you, with the possibility of a fine or jail sentence.

The principle here is that parties to a suit have the right to compel anyone who knows facts material to the case to come to court and testify. Thus, the physician who treats the victim of a car crash is subject to the same legalities as the plumber who saw the car slam into a tree. In fact, the treating doctor who fails to testify in such a case may leave himself open to more than a contempt citation; the patient just might be able to recover damages from him. Consider the following instance:

A New Jersey doctor treated a woman injured in an auto accident. When she sued the other driver, the doctor agreed to testify in her behalf. For some unexplained reason, however, he didn't appear in court at the designated time. Damages were awarded to the woman, but they were much less than they probably would have been if the doctor had testified for her. The court held that the woman had a good cause of action for breach of contract against the doctor.

While a physician can't refuse to go to court if he's subpoenaed, he *can* object if the subpoena is too broadly worded. I once argued in favor of a doctor who'd been served with a subpoena directing him to bring "all and sundry . . . files, papers, documents, and instruments in your office concerned with all the cases you have handled involving fractures." Since this would have greatly inconvenienced the doctor, and since only a few of the documents demanded were pertinent to the case, I filed an application to the trial judge to suppress the subpoena or have it modified.

In my application, I cited a ruling of the Supreme Court of Wisconsin that held: "No doubt the witness may, before he is required to answer, have the determination of a court as to whether or not the matters as to which it is proposed to examine him are material and relevant to the controversy. This is particularly true where he is required to exhibit books and papers relating to matters other than those appertaining to the facts in dispute."

I won my point. The way-out subpoena was knocked down, and the doctor was required to furnish only a few papers that were relevant to the case.

2. If you're requested to appear as an "expert" witness—one prepared to offer opinions on the medical issues involved—you can accept or decline as you choose. Before deciding, it's advisable to ask the lawyer concerned (1) what medical theory he wants you to prove, and (2) what facts he has to back it up. If you have any doubts about the facts fitting the theory, you should decline to testify as an expert witness. At best, the case has questionable merit; at worst, someone may be trying to make you a party to a trumped-up claim.

Oh, yes, such things do happen. Many doctors who've worked in hospital emergency departments are aware of touts who seek prospective clients for lawyers. One brazen fellow used to show up at Midwest hospitals wearing a clerical collar and carrying a Bible. In this guise, he gained access to injured patients, commiserated with them, then left the card of a "wonderful attorney" who could do a "great job" of exacting damages from the villain in the case.

Sometimes an unscrupulous accident victim doesn't need to be touted into litigation. He develops "compensation neurosis," an affliction that can be cured only by a sizable award, otherwise known as a "greenback poultice."

Doctors who appear—through carelessness or misplaced sympathy—as expert medical witnesses for such charlatans run the risk of acute embarrassment or worse. One physician, for example, backed up the story of a man who claimed he'd been rendered impotent by an injury in the scrotal area. After winning a whopping award, our injured man jubilantly went on to sire seven offspring.

In another case, a "nice little old lady" convinced a doctor that her multiplicity of back ailments were all due to a bus accident. And he so testified in court. The defense then introduced more than 200 pages of hospital records, showing that the "nice little old lady's" back ailments had been receiving extensive treatment for many years prior to the bus accident.

Before agreeing to appear as an expert medical witness, therefore, make sure the case you're supporting is solidly based. Make sure, too, that you do your homework before going to court. I'll advise you on how to do that in the following chapter.

III

YOU CAN'T GO WRONG WITH THE RIGHT PREPARATION

During a newspaper interview, a famous judge was asked what was necessary to win a court trial.

"First you need a good case," he replied; "then you need good witnesses; then you need a good judge; then you need a good jury; and then you need good luck."

Professional diffidence deters me from dwelling on the fact that His Honor neglected to mention the need for a good lawyer. However, I must emphatically point out another omission from his list: The necessity of adequately preparing those "good witnesses," especially the expert medical witnesses.

Of all the failings that get doctors into difficulties on the witness stand, lack of the right kind of preparation is the most damaging. In all fairness, I'll admit that some lawyers contribute to this failing. They tell the medical witness, "Just get up there on the stand and tell the truth, and you'll be a winner." That's like a baseball coach telling a batter, "Just go up to the plate and swing hard, and you'll hit a home run." Obviously something more is needed. Before a medical witness takes the stand, there are six points of preparation he should work out with the lawyer who has requested that he give testimony. The first is:

III 1. *What kind of witness am I to be?* Basically, there are two kinds of medical witness—the "fact" type and the "opinion" type.

The "fact" witness is usually called to testify about the medical condition of a patient he's treated. In general, his testimony will include the medical history of the patient, results of tests and examinations, the diagnosis, the treatment, the present condition, and possibly a prognosis.

The "opinion" witness is called as an expert to help the court reach conclusions on the medical issues in the case. He's allowed to express opinions based not only on the facts of the case, but on his own observations and knowledge of similar cases.

It's entirely possible for a doctor to testify as an expert medical witness without having examined the patient, or even having personal experience in the type of injury or ailment involved. In an Ohio case, for example, a medical expert testified that in his opinion a brewery worker had been blinded by fumes from varnish with which he was working. Lawyers for the brewery objected; they claimed the witness had never treated a case of that kind, and consequently his opinion should not be considered expert. The court ruled otherwise. It held that the witness had done enough scientific investigation in this medical area to qualify as an expert.

It's best, however, that an expert witness examine the patient before the trial. In one case I remember well, a cross-examiner greatly diminished the value of a medical expert's testimony by making remarks such as: "But of course you've never examined the patient," and "It's wonderful, Doctor, how you can reach such an opinion without having so much as spoken to the patient."

To obviate such prejudicial remarks, therefore, the expert medical witness should insist on examining the patient. Failing that, he should be armed with a good reason to explain why the patient can't, or won't, be examined.

YOU CAN'T GO WRONG WITH THE RIGHT PREPARATION

If a long period of time intervenes between a medical examination and the trial, another checkup is advisable. The patient's condition may have changed considerably, as Melvin M. Belli, the noted California attorney, discovered on one occasion. He was representing an attractive widow whose husband had been killed in an automobile accident. Belli's plan was to place her on the witness stand and bring out how inconsolably bereaved she was by the loss of her husband. There was, however, a delay of almost two years before the case came up on the court calendar. Three days before the trial, Belli called in the widow for a conference. He took one look at her and reached for the phone to start negotiations for an out-of-court settlement. The "bereaved" widow was so pregnant, as Belli later put it, that "she might have produced an offspring on the witness stand."

2. *Is it ethical for me to plan the strategy of a case with a lawyer?* It's not only ethical, it's a moral necessity. Only by amassing all the medical truth of a claim can justice be truly served. The American Medical Association has this to say on the subject: "*Do* insist on preparation for your testimony in consultation with the attorney for the party who called you as a witness. He should advise you on what to expect on cross-examination. You have a right to consult with the party and his attorney about the case, so don't be embarrassed if asked about such consultation." Dr. Cyril H. Wecht, whom we quoted in Chapter I, adds:

"Some doctors get flustered on the stand when they're asked if they've discussed the case with anyone. They shouldn't. There's no conspiracy involved, and the cross-examiner knows that. His sole purpose is to rattle the witness. The doctor should simply answer, 'Yes.' If asked with whom he discussed the case, he should name the attorney. The usual question then is, 'And you talked about the testimony you'd give in court, didn't you, Doctor?' The correct reply is: 'We talked about the substance of the medical matters involved, and we discussed how we could most clearly present the information to the jury.' "

3. *How do I fit into the case?* The best way is to assume the role of teacher. Point out to the attorney the medical features most likely to enlighten the jury, and together you decide on the most effective way to present them.

"The method I use," says one of the best expert medical witnesses I know, "is to think of my testimony as a well-structured story. I start off with a 'grabber,' something to catch the interest of the jury. For instance, in a case a few years ago, a young man was suing a bus company—both his legs had been seriously injured in a crash. As I'd arranged with his lawyer, the first question put to me was, 'Doctor, medically speaking, what can this young man look forward to?' 'Life in a wheelchair,' I replied. 'In my opinion, he'll never walk again.'

"It was an arresting remark. In fact, you could see shock and sympathy reflected in the faces of the jurors—but it was the truth. The lawyer and I then went into the essential medical aspects of the case. We built point upon point of interest, each one mounting until we reached the climax of our presentation—a detailed account in plain English of the many fractured and broken bones this man had sustained in the crash. He was awarded damages of almost $500,000."

While an attorney is naturally interested in learning from a medical witness the favorable aspects of a case, he also wants to know anything unfavorable that might cause trouble. I found out the hard way that medical witnesses don't always volunteer this information. In one of my earliest cases, I had a kindly old country doctor as a witness. On the stand, under my direct examination, he backed up my case beautifully. Then, to my horror, on cross-examination he conceded damaging medical points of which I wasn't aware.

YOU CAN'T GO WRONG WITH THE RIGHT PREPARATION

Afterward I said to him with some exasperation, "Doctor, why didn't you tell me those unfavorable things?" Said the doctor in mild reproof, "Jack, you didn't ask me."

Well, I've been sure to ask ever since. However, if a lawyer you work with should neglect to question you on whether there are weak medical spots in a case, it's in your own best interests to bring them up. Both you and the lawyer could look bad if these points are brought out on cross-examination in court. When the lawyer knows about them in advance, he can minimize their effect. One good way is for him to take them up on direct examination. This not only spikes the guns of the cross-examiner, but enhances the credibility of the witness.

It's also advisable for an expert witness to anticipate what medical theory the opposition will try to put across. Then the doctor can help the lawyer to plan a counter-attack.

4. *Should I rehearse what I'm going to say on the stand?* Not the exact words, but certainly you should marshal the necessary facts and go over the *ideas* you want to present. You and the lawyer can then arrange them in effective sequence.

I find as a lawyer that another useful preliminary is to draft key questions and put them to the doctor, thus giving him an advance opportunity to shape his answers. Most important, I include questions that may be asked on cross-examination.

Sometime during the pretrial conference the doctor should tell the lawyer the principal medical terms he intends to use. This serves two purposes: It enables the lawyer to select scientific terms that the doctor should translate into plain English for the jury, and it familiarizes the lawyer with words that might be difficult for him to pronounce.

III In a Midwest trial not long ago, one lawyer consistently mispronounced ecchymosis. The first thing the opposition lawyer did on cross-examination of the medical witness was to get him to give the correct pronunciation of the word. The medical witness, in effect, was used to make the lawyer for his side look silly in the eyes of the jury. Not that one juror in a million could himself pronounce ecchymosis, but in a courtroom it's always better for one's own lawyer to be laughed with, rather than laughed at.

5. *What reading should I do before taking the stand?* Pertinent medical records, documents, and reports are a must. It's also wise to consult key textbooks and review the literature on the medical problem involved, especially when authorities agree with the opinion you will present in court. Conversely, if the witness is aware that some authorities have different opinions, he should be prepared to explain the reason for his position.

James A. Brussel, the noted psychiatrist who's testified as an expert medical witness many times, reads the literature for what he calls "the exception." His reason for this goes back to 1936. In a case that year, a certain type of blood test on a woman who claimed to be a virgin showed she had syphilis. Brussel, who believed the woman's claim, went over the literature on that type of blood test. In a clinical journal he came across just the article he wanted. The author wrote that people who'd had black measles when young would always check out as having syphilis under the blood test used on the woman. She had, it turned out, suffered with black measles when she was a child. However dubious this piece of information may seem today, when Brussel went on the stand with it, he scored heavily.

6. *What else do I need to do or know before testifying?* If you're due to appear in an unfamiliar courthouse, it's helpful to visit the place for a few minutes and look

around, just as in many hospitals today, patients facing certain procedures are given advance tours of the premises to help them relieve their uneasiness.

YOU CAN'T GO WRONG WITH THE RIGHT PREPARATION

If you can't visit the courthouse, have the lawyer you're working with give you specific details of its layout. He might even draw you a diagram, as I do for medical witnesses appearing in a court for the first time. Also—and this is very important—be sure the lawyer informs you whether you're to go directly into the courtroom and wait your turn as a witness, or whether you must remain outside until you're called. If a motion to exclude is made before the actual trial starts, it must be granted in most states and the judge must exclude from the courtroom all witnesses except the one who's testifying. If you were to barge in under those conditions, a mistrial might be declared.

Whenever a doctor-witness is unfamiliar with trial procedure in a civil action, I give him an A-B-C rundown on what to expect:

A. The trial usually begins with an opening statement to the jury by the plaintiff's counsel. The opening statement by the defense lawyer follows. Both attorneys outline what they intend to prove.

B. Testimony and evidence are presented by the plaintiff to support his claims. The defense tries to counter these contentions by offering testimony and evidence of its own. Rebuttals by the plaintiff and the defense may follow if necessary. The point at which the doctor-witness appears, of course, depends on whether he's testifying for the plaintiff or the defense.

C. The attorneys address their concluding arguments to the jury. The trial judge instructs the jury, and the jury then retires to consider the case.

If you're the defendant in a malpractice case, your insurance carrier will provide a lawyer. Most of these attorneys are experienced and able. Beware, however, of the lawyer who's inclined to "wing it," with only sketchy preparation. Demand that he prepare you. Ask him questions. Insist on consultations.

If he's not cooperative, or if he seems to be more concerned about the carrier's interests than yours, or if you just don't feel comfortable with him, you may want to get your own backup attorney. In that case, don't settle for someone who's a general practitioner, or who has had little or no trial experience. Retain a lawyer who has a proven record in medico-legal matters. Your local medical society can probably recommend someone.

Even then, check out the lawyer yourself. Question him about his methods of preparation for the trial. Two questions are particularly important:

1. *Is he preparing for what the plaintiff's side might do?* This sort of anticipation is vital. I was once called into a malpractice case just three days before the trial. The plaintiff's lawyer had suddenly increased the damages demanded to more than five times the amount of the defendant doctor's malpractice coverage. In other words, if he lost the suit, he might have had to pay up to $750,000 out of his own pocket.

Ordinarily I would never have taken a case on such short notice. But the defendant was a friend of mine, he was desperate, and I felt I had to try to help him. With the assistance of several of my younger associates, I went over the defense drawn up by the insurance attorney.

It was lacking in two respects: No thought had been given to what the other side would do, and only one, rather inadequate, expert medical witness had been retained.

I won't go into the details, but this was an extremely complex case. It required at least three expert witnesses, each an authority in a specific field of medicine. Through various contacts—and with a lot of luck—I was able to obtain the three experts.

The defendant-doctor and I sat down with them. One

of the main questions I asked was, "What would you say about the medical features of this case if you were appearing for the plaintiff?"

YOU CAN'T GO WRONG WITH THE RIGHT PREPARATION

The points they brought up were consolidated in a brief to oppose the probable claims the plaintiff's side would present during the trial. The insurance attorney and I, along with my young associates, then set up a combined defense strategy.

It worked to some extent. After deliberating for two days, the jury brought back a verdict against my client. But the amount of the award was less than one-third of the doctor's policy limit. He had been saved from financial ruin.

I still think we could have won that case if we'd had adequate time for preparation.

2. *Is your lawyer including you sufficiently in the preparation of the case?* Keep in mind that an attorney is not nearly as knowledgeable about medicine as you are. He's going to need your assistance. Go over all the clinical matters involved, and make sure the lawyer understands them. And bring up points that might help in your defense.

Some of these tips can be surprisingly simple, yet wonderfully effective. In one case, my client suggested that we visit the surgical suite where the operation in question had been performed. With permission of the hospital administration, the surgeon and I carefully went over every aspect of the operation, right on the spot where it had all happened.

This had three particularly good effects: It refreshed the doctor's recollection and enabled him to supply me with additional details. It gave me a clearer picture of what had occurred. And it brought the doctor and me into closer rapport and cooperation. We worked so well together at the trial that the judge stopped it at midpoint and directed a verdict for the surgeon.

In another case, a client of mine was accused of bungling a hysterectomy. The patient claimed that after she was discharged from the hospital, she noticed bits of tissue in the toilet after she voided. The doctor, she charged, had negligently failed to remove all the tissue.

During one of my conferences with the doctor, he remarked, "You know, you might check with the Association of Visiting Nurses."

"What have they got to do with it?" I asked.

"I referred the patient to them. I thought she might need post-op attention, and she didn't seem to want to come back to me."

I then contacted the nursing association and asked if the plaintiff had followed through on the referral. She hadn't. Through two expert witnesses, I ascertained that the woman had been the victim of her own negligence. She had suffered from epithelial sloughing incident to cystitis that had developed, at least in part, because of her lack of personal cleanliness and proper douching.

The doctor won the case—largely, I'm sure, because he pointed me in the right direction to obtain the evidence we needed.

One last item on preparation:

During a trial many years ago, while I was questioning a medical witness at length, I noticed that he was squirming on the stand in a particularly distressful way. I suddenly realized that the poor fellow's bladder must be bursting. After some suspenseful verbal parrying with the judge and the opposition lawyer, I managed to arrange a brief recess. I then hustled my medical witness off to what was quaintly but aptly known in those days as a comfort station. Ever since then, if a witness is unfamiliar with a courthouse, I let him know where the rest room is and suggest that he use it before appearing in court.

If you prepare properly, and play your cards right, you might be able to testify without appearing in court at all. That is explained in the next chapter.

WILL YOUR DEPOSITION TRAP YOU?

IV

Because giving a deposition at a pretrial hearing is so informal a proceeding, the unwary medical witness can easily slip into some dangerous pitfalls. First of all, too many doctors try to resist giving such pretrial testimony in civil cases. They ignore summonses, or they call the lawyer concerned and try to wriggle out of appearing.

In some instances, a doctor will get tough. "I'm too busy to appear, and I'm *not going* to appear!" he declares. The next thing he knows, he's hauled before a judge and held in contempt of court—and after all that, he still has to appear to give his deposition.

Experienced medical witnesses know better than to make that mistake. But that's only one of many ways a doctor can get into trouble over a deposition. Of all the legal procedures in civil actions, the deposition is probably the most misunderstood. The main reason is this: A deposition is taken at a pretrial hearing held away from the courtroom, and thus seems removed from the majesty and authority of the law. In fact, the medical witness who's called upon for a deposition is subject to all the responsibilities and penalties of testifying in court.

Nevertheless, the deposition is more of a boon than a bane to a medical witness. Instead of fighting a summons to appear at such a pretrial hearing, the doctor should welcome it. Properly handled, the deposition may free him from appearing in court. We'll go into that later. First, though, let's look at the mechanics of the deposition and see where dangers lurk for the unwary physician—who, incidentally, can be the veteran medical witness as well as the novice.

The purpose of the deposition is to acquaint both sides in certain civil cases with the facts and arguments that will be presented in court. It may seem incongruous for two contestants in a legal action to reveal their secrets to each other. As the law sees it, however, if unexpected testimony were to catch one or the other side by surprise during the trial, an injustice might result. So, to give both sides a fair opportunity to prepare rebuttals to all contentions, depositions of the key witnesses are taken over a period of time in advance of the trial.

Deposition proceedings are highly informal. They can be held just about anywhere—including, in one instance I've heard about, the back room of a tavern. More often than not, though, the setting is a lawyer's office.

Let's say a doctor is summoned for a deposition in behalf of the plaintiff in a personal injury suit. Both lawyers in the case are on hand, and the attorney for the plaintiff is allowed to offer the witness advice and assistance. The only other person who must be present is a stenographer, who records everything. There's no judge. Just as in court, however, the witness may undergo both direct and cross-examination, and his testimony is taken under oath.

One of the most important things to keep in mind about a deposition is that any or all of it can be introduced during the actual trial. Consequently, if a medical witness says one thing during the deposition and another in court, he's in trouble. In a case several years ago, for example, a doctor declared on the witness stand that the plaintiff's epileptic seizures were the direct result of head injuries received in a car crash. The defense lawyer then read from a deposition in which the same doctor had said that epilepsy was not likely to occur.

The doctor tried to excuse himself on the grounds that his initial examination of the plaintiff had been hasty, and that his deposition had been given more than a year previously and he'd forgotten what he'd said then. The jury was not favorably impressed. A doctor who's forced to admit to a hasty examination is suspect; and a doctor who doesn't study the testimony he gave in a deposition more than a year previously is certainly not as thorough-going as a doctor should be.

The moral: If you don't remember exactly what you said in your deposition, read a copy of it before going into court. If there *are* discrepancies between what you said at the deposition hearing and what you intend to say on the witness stand, be sure that you have good reasons for the differences.

Sometimes, especially in large cities, as much as five years can go by between the deposition and the trial, and medical thought—and your opinion—might change in that time. In that case, the opposition attorney may well pose the following question: "Is your testimony here today, Doctor, in conflict with your deposition?"

Your answer should simply be, "Yes." The lawyer on whose side you're testifying will have a chance on redirect examination to straighten out the apparent conflict. Therefore, be prepared to explain the change in medical thought.

It's an absolute must to review your deposition before trial. I well remember a radiologist who appeared for the plaintiff in a malpractice case. I represented the defendant doctor. Three years had transpired between the radiologist's deposition and the trial.

On the stand, the radiologist testified that he had

recommended a laminectomy for the patient. I then pointed out that in his deposition he had diagnosed a herniated disc and had said a stout supporting garment, like a corset, would control the problem.

The radiologist, who obviously had not reviewed his deposition, was at first flustered. He kept muttering things like, "It's been so long ago. . . . How can I be expected to remember everything?"

He became angry when I pressed him for an explanation of the differences in his opinions. At one point, he had a shadow box brought into court to examine the X-rays, but that didn't satisfy him. He jumped up and held the X-rays against a window behind the witness box.

Although he was a highly reputable, board-certified specialist, he looked like an amateur to the jury.

On redirect examination, the plaintiff's lawyer tried to imply that either a corset or a laminectomy would have been consistent with established procedure.

On recross-examination, I asked the radiologist only one question: "Doctor, isn't it true that in your pretrial, sworn deposition, you referred only to a supportive corset, not surgery?"

He fumbled around for a bit, but finally came up with a weak, "Yes." His side lost the case—partly, I think, because the witness hadn't reviewed his deposition and prepared himself accordingly.

It's also essential for a doctor to prepare for giving a deposition just as carefully as he'd prepare for a court appearance. Testimony at the pretrial stage can be just as important as testimony in court—and possibly *more* important.

A West Coast internist learned that lesson during a personal injury case. The internist was vague and casual during questioning at the deposition hearing. He hadn't even bothered to review his records, and he admitted he was "guessing" as to the extent of the plaintiff's injuries.

At the trial, the internist was much more exact in his testimony. Nevertheless, its value was greatly diminished when excerpts from the deposition were introduced. The witness not only damaged the case for the plaintiff by not properly preparing for the deposition, he also hurt himself. The trial was widely reported in the press and on television and radio, and the internist definitely didn't emerge as a thoroughly trustworthy professional.

The trap that the internist fell into—the feeling that a deposition is too informal to be taken seriously—is a common one. At some pretrial hearings, the atmosphere is extremely relaxed. The lawyers involved may be friends in private life. Whereas in court they might be at each other's throats, they're now inquiring about each other's families and perhaps sipping coffee. Under those circumstances, it's easy for the medical witness to let his guard down. And that can be disastrous.

That's exactly how it turned out when, during a deposition in a Southern state, an orthopedist lightly remarked that a patient he'd examined "seemed to be a crybaby." The remark was read back to him in court. He tried to explain that he was simply saying the patient had a low pain threshold, but the jury eyed him dubiously. Laymen are suspicious of doctors who sound callous.

Another thing I've noticed about depositions: If the participants are all men and a sexual element is involved in the case under discussion, a bawdy air sometimes creeps in. When that happens, beware: Off-color wisecracks are contagious. If someone in a group of men gets one off, others are greatly tempted to top it. For example, consider what happened in the following case:

An Eastern urologist was giving his deposition. The lawyers in the case were convivial, and the medical complaint of the plaintiff was conducive to coarse humor. He had priapism, the condition in which the penis remains constantly erect. The urologist explained that the condition occurs in some cases of lymphatic and myogenous leukemia, and in patients with disease or injury of the spine or spinal cord.

He should have stopped there. Instead, because the lawyers were wisecracking, the urologist couldn't resist contributing one of his own. "On the other hand," he remarked of the plaintiff, "maybe the guy is just horny!"

That got a laugh—but not when it was read in court. The jury didn't think it was a laughing matter after they'd heard evidence that the plaintiff was unable to urinate satisfactorily, that he had to have catheter drainage, and that suprapubic cystotomy was being considered. To say the urologist was embarrassed is putting it mildly.

Although a medical witness is obliged to answer relevant questions during a deposition, he should be wary of divulging information about a patient that has no bearing on the case. Usually, the lawyer for the doctor's side will restrain him from this blunder, but sometimes the lawyer slips up. That's what happened some years ago to J. L. Bordenave, an Illinois family physician. A patient of his, a married woman, had been injured in an auto accident. During a deposition, at which the woman and her husband were present, it came out that she had consulted Dr. Bordenave a short time before the accident occurred.

When asked to reveal why the woman had consulted him, the physician declined, saying it had no relevance to the accident. The opposition lawyer insisted, however, and—surprisingly—the woman's own attorney put up no objection.

"So in the presence of the woman and her husband, the lawyers, and a court reporter, I disclosed that she'd come to me because she was worried about being frigid," says Dr. Bordenave. "I was later told by a judge I know that I didn't have to volunteer irrelevant information sought in a 'fishing expedition' by the questioner. Not so incidentally, I never again saw the couple as patients, and I've often wondered what effect the needless revelation had on their marriage."

Now let's look at the bright side of the deposition process. Since the hearing needn't fit into a court calendar, the time and place can be adjusted to suit the convenience of those involved. Some medical witnesses don't realize this. They grumble about what they consider an imposition, and put themselves out to attend the deposition proceedings. This can usually be avoided by a simple phone call to the lawyer concerned. Almost invariably, he'll be glad to set a time convenient for the medical witness.

That's not all. As I've said earlier, a medical witness is a kind of dignitary. Most lawyers are only too willing to accommodate him. Therefore, if you'd prefer to have a deposition held in your own office, say so. This is often arranged.

The best way to save yourself time and trouble is to come to the hearing well prepared, then give your testimony with all the expertise and seriousness that you'd muster in court. Both sides may be so impressed that they'll agree to accept your statements just as you've given them. This means that the deposition will be introduced at the trial, but you won't have to attend.

A good performance by a medical witness while giving a deposition can also keep a case from ever going to trial. The plaintiff's lawyer may see that his case isn't as good as he thought, or the defense lawyer may be reluctant to take on such a formidable medical witness before a judge and jury. Negotiations may then result in a settlement, a result that spares the medical witness a time-consuming date in the courtroom.

Whether a medical witness appears in court or not, however, the question of his fee remains. We'll go into that and related questions next.

HOW TO FIGURE A WITNESS FEE

V

How much are you entitled to charge as a medical witness? Who will pay you? How can you make sure you'll get paid? Even veteran medical witnesses aren't always certain—and for good reason. The courts aren't consistent in matters relating to fees for medical witnesses.

For example, in an Alabama case some years ago, a physician was called to testify about wounds that had allegedly caused the death of a patient. After he had described the wounds, he was asked what their probable effect had been. The doctor declined to answer on the grounds that he hadn't been paid to give a professional opinion, nor had a promise to pay been made. The judge ordered him to testify, but the witness still refused. He was then fined for contempt of court, a ruling that was later upheld by the Alabama Supreme Court.

In a similar case, however, an opposite view was taken by the Indiana Supreme Court: A doctor had been summoned as a fact witness, and was asked to give a medical opinion. When he refused, he was jailed for contempt of court. Setting aside the commitment order, the state's high court declared:

"While a physician or surgeon could be required to attend as witness to facts, without other compensation than that provided by law for other witnesses, yet he could not be required to testify as to his professional opinion without the compensation of a professional fee. The professional knowledge of a . . . physician is to be regarded in the light of property, and his professional services are no more at the mercy of the public, as to remuneration, than are the goods of the merchant, or the crops of the farmer, or the wares of the mechanic."

Those two rulings highlight a couple of important points. First, a courtroom is hardly the place to start making a fuss about a witness fee. A medical witness who has any question about the fee he's to receive should settle the matter with the lawyer concerned before going to court. Secondly, a number of states do have laws that can compel a medical witness to testify under some circumstances for a minimal fee or nothing at all. In general, however, the following guidelines apply: If a doctor is appearing as an opinion witness, he can set his own fee—within reason, of course. If the doctor is testifying as a fact witness, he's technically entitled only to the basic witness fee.

That doesn't mean that the medical fact witness is always stuck with the paltry standard fee. If his testimony is vital to a case, and if he must spend considerable time in reviewing records and appearing in court, it's not uncommon for the lawyer involved to offer appropriate compensation. If the lawyer doesn't make the offer, the doctor is entitled to raise the fee question.

Sometimes the doctor summoned as a medical fact witness is also expected to express medical opinions on the stand. In that case, he has good grounds for requesting more than the basic fee.

The purely factual witness should keep in mind that if he refuses to testify, because of a fee dispute or for any other reason, he can be forced to appear in court by subpoena. This doesn't happen often, for a very good reason: The lawyer doesn't want a sullen, unfriendly medical witness on his hands.

HOW TO FIGURE A WITNESS FEE

In any event, the doctor should ascertain *before* going to court which witness category he's in and on what basis he's to be paid. I know of an internist who was summoned to testify about an elderly patient of his who had died. The physician spent quite some time going back through the patient's medical records and boning up on the details of her various ailments. He also spent time toting up his witness fee, which he figured should come to at least $500.

Then he steeled himself for the rigors of a tough, lengthy courtroom examination. On the stand, however, he was asked a single question: "Did you ever see the patient's brother taking care of her?" When the doctor said, "Yes," he was dismissed. The case, it turned out, concerned a will the brother was contesting, and the doctor had been called only to corroborate the man's claim that he'd nursed the patient. The internist received an ordinary witness fee of $25, plus a 60-cent-per-mile travel allowance.

When a doctor knows for sure that he's to appear as an expert medical witness—that is, to express medical opinions—another question comes up: What's a good way to figure the fee? Some doctors set a lump sum, but there are drawbacks to that: If it's low, and the doctor has to put in more time than he expected, he comes out on the short end. If it's high, it can cause complications in court. For example, I remember an orthopedist who was asked by a cross-examiner: "What are you being paid for testifying?"

The doctor hesitated, then turned to the judge and asked, "Do I have to answer that?"

The judge told him that he did, and the orthopedist said he was being paid $1,500. The cross-examiner appeared to be shocked. He consulted his wristwatch and exclaimed: "That's mighty good pay for a man who's been on the stand for less than half an hour! No more questions—you're dismissed, Doctor."

The orthopedist had made the following mistakes:

○ He'd responded to a question that was phrased to make it sound as though he was selling his testimony. The correct answer would have been: "I'm not being paid anything for my testimony. I'm being paid for my time, my professional knowledge, my services in studying the medical facts in this case, and for my medical opinions based on those facts."

○ He'd appeared reluctant to reveal the amount of his fee, thus giving the impression that he was trying to hide something. Actually, more often than not, an expert medical witness will be questioned on the stand about his fee, and he should be prepared to answer promptly and willingly.

○ He'd set his fee at the lump sum of $1,500. This may well have been legitimate, but it had a souring effect on members of the jury who might have to labor a month or more to make $1,500.

Therefore, it's generally best for an expert medical witness to compute his fee on an hourly basis. Most physicians know what they average in an hour of treating patients, and this can be used as a starting point in figuring a witness fee. I'm speaking of gross hourly income, of course, since a doctor's practice expenses continue while he's working on a court case.

Also take into consideration your professional training and expertise, plus any complexities that may be involved in the case. Those may place special value on your testimony.

Do *not* base your fee on rates that other doctors tell you they charge for testifying. If you do, you just might find yourself facing legal action stemming from the antitrust provisions of the Sherman Act.

Oddly enough, there are expert medical witnesses who charge a high hourly fee, yet cheat themselves in other ways. I recall a professionally able specialist who for years was a great favorite of lawyers—the reason: He charged only for the time spent in court.

In fact, an expert medical witness is entitled to charge for the time spent and expenses incurred in making out reports, attending pretrial conferences, doing research, giving testimony at deposition hearings, *and* appearing in court. If the doctor has to travel to another town and stay overnight for the trial, he should arrange for the costs of transportation, hotel room, meals, and tips to be paid. If the attorney or the party he represents cancels an appointment on short notice, the doctor has a right to include in his fee the value of the time he's lost.

When the doctor has provided considerable pretrial medical care to the party concerned in litigation, it's generally best to keep those charges separate from the witness fee. For one thing, such bills must be submitted to the jury as part of the claimant's medical expenses. For another, if the patient is insured the doctor can routinely submit his bills to the carrier or its attorney. That not only protects the doctor against possible loss, it also strengthens the case of the claimant. A jury gives more weight to the testimony of a doctor who's already been paid than to the testimony of one who's still awaiting payment of his charges for preparing for and giving testimony. Why? Because the jury may infer that the latter's fee is going to depend on the outcome of the trial.

It's unethical, of course, for a medical witness to enter into any agreement that makes his fee contingent on the outcome of a trial. In North Carolina, a doctor-witness who had asked for and received a percentage of a damages award was ordered by a court to repay the money. Similarly, in New York, an attorney was disbarred for negotiating an agreement that would have paid a medical witness a substantial share of any damages that might have been awarded in a personal injury case.

While a medical witness can't agree to a contingent fee arrangement, he can make exceptions as to how he's to be paid. If a patient is indigent, for example, a doctor can ethically agree to serve as a medical witness without guarantee of payment. In that case, he should bill the patient as usual, but with the knowledge that he might not be paid. If the patient is awarded damages, chances are he'll honor his debt to the doctor.

One note of caution: While the doctor is on the stand, he should be prepared to rebut any insinuation of contingency. To downgrade the doctor's testimony, the cross-examiner might bring out the fact that his bill hasn't been paid and suggest that it won't be paid unless the case is won. The correct response to that sort of suggestion is: "There has been no such arrangement. The bill is still owed whether the case is won or lost. In fact, I have many patients who don't pay their bills." If the cross-examiner persists, the doctor can cite the actual percentage of his bills that aren't paid.

Here's another trap to watch for: If the medical witness is basing his fee on his average hourly gross earnings, the cross-examiner may try to have him estimate his total fee, hoping it will add up to a huge sum. A good comeback to this ploy is: "My total fee depends on how long you keep me here."

Whom should the doctor bill for his services as an expert medical witness? Usually, he's paid through the lawyer who calls upon him to testify. The doctor, however, should also send statements to the lawyer's client, who in most cases is ultimately responsible for paying the medical witness's fee. The attorney has no obligation to pay the fee unless he specifically agrees to do so, or guarantees that his client will pay.

HOW TO FIGURE A WITNESS FEE

To make sure there's no misunderstanding about who's to pay and how much is to be paid, the fee should be agreed upon before the doctor enters the case. If the doctor knows the lawyer or claimant, an oral agreement is usually sufficient. Otherwise, it's best to get the agreement in writing. This can take the form of an exchange of letters between the lawyer and the doctor. The lawyer's letter should read something like this:

> *In behalf of my client, John Doe, I herewith request that you prepare yourself to testify as an expert medical witness in the case of Doe v. Roe, scheduled to come to trial in such-and-such court at such-and-such time.*
>
> *My client and I realize, of course, that you will have to study the medical problems involved, make reports, attend pretrial conferences or hearings, provide me with medical advice, and arrive at your medical opinions, as well as testify about them in court. I agree in behalf of my client that you will be paid for time spent on these preparations and services at the rate of $ ______ an hour. I also agree in behalf of my client that you will be compensated for any expenses you may incur in providing these services.*
>
> *In the event that the case is settled out of court, I agree in behalf of my client that you will be compensated for preparations and services provided by you up to the point of settlement.*

Let me emphasize the importance of that last paragraph, since many civil cases never get to court. Unless the medical witness has an agreement that he's to be paid for his preparations and services regardless of whether he testifies in court, he may end up empty-handed.

Does a doctor have to wait until a case is over before he gets paid for his services as an expert medical witness? Not necessarily. If there's a considerable time lag before the case goes to trial, he can request payment for services as he provides them. If it's known how long he'll be needed in court, he can also request payment in advance. The claimant may not be able to pay, but many lawyers make advances in behalf of their clients for certain litigation fees.

If an attorney should ever tell you that this isn't ethical, you might quote to him Canon 42 of the American Bar Association's Canons of Judicial Ethics. It states that while a lawyer may not properly agree with a client that the attorney should bear the expenses of litigation, the lawyer *can* ethically advance expenses as a matter of convenience, subject to reimbursement.

Even though the attorney is unwilling or unable to advance the full fee of a medical witness, he may compromise by providing a retainer. In that case, the letter from the lawyer should contain another paragraph: "You will be paid $ ______ as a retainer. This sum is to be credited on any bill submitted by you to my client for the services you have been asked to render."

In reply to the lawyer, the doctor need only send a letter stating: "I agree to provide services for your client, John Doe, on the terms and for the purposes that were specified in your letter dated ______ ."

Those two letters constitute an enforceable contract. Unhappily, that doesn't always mean that the medical witness will get paid. In some instances, if he's waited until the outcome of the trial for payment, and if the verdict has gone against the claimant, the doctor may have trouble collecting his fee. In that event, if the lawyer has agreed to pay the fee, or has guaranteed that it will be paid, the doctor can complain either to the local bar association, or to the medico-legal committee of the county medical society. That usually does the trick; no lawyer wants a bad reputation among doctors, especially an attorney who needs medical witnesses.

Even if the lawyer hasn't guaranteed the fee, the doctor can ask him to use his influence to get his client to pay. The lawyer is usually in a better position to do this than the doctor is.

If that doesn't work, the doctor can turn the bill over to a collection agency. As a last resort, he can sue for the money owed him. The expert medical witness will seldom have fee trouble if he reaches a clear understanding in advance on what he's to be paid, when it's to be paid, and who's to pay it.

If you're the defendant in a medico-legal case and need an expert witness, you can help your attorney obtain the right specialist. How to do that is the subject of the next chapter.

PICKING THE RIGHT EXPERT WITNESS

VI

Here's part of the transcript from a medical malpractice trial. On the stand is an expert witness for the defendant. The plaintiff's attorney is questioning him.

Q. When you were in medical school, did you know the defendant?
A. Yes.
Q. In fact, you were roommates?
A. Yes.
Q. How long ago was that?
A. Oh—about 25 years.
Q. Since then, have you been associated with the defendant?
A. In what way?
Q. Well, professionally. Have you covered for him—has he covered for you?
A. Oh, yes.
Q. Often?
A. Quite often.
Q. And, socially, do you and your wife often get together with the defendant and his wife?
A. Yes.
Q. In fact, Doctor, would you say you're a close friend of the defendant?

A. Yes.

Q. And you've been close friends for the past 25 years?

A. Yes.

Q. Thank you, Doctor. That will be all.

Now, that expert witness was a highly qualified specialist. Ordinarily his testimony would have carried considerable weight. In this case, it was rendered virtually worthless when the plaintiff's attorney brought out the long and close association between the two doctors.

So if you're the defendant in a malpractice case, don't call in a close friend as an expert witness. That doesn't mean you shouldn't use physicians you may know through professional contacts. Just make sure the association isn't so close that it will cast doubt on the expert's testimony.

Here are five other major points to keep in mind when you and your attorney are considering expert witnesses.

1. *Is the physician fully qualified?* In other words, does he know what he's talking about? Can he demonstrate to a jury that he has the training and experience to support his medical opinions? Is he professionally recognized by his peers? Is he board certified? Is he a member of meaningful professional associations, such as the American College of Surgeons?

If the answers are all "Yes," that's a good start—but it may not be all. The qualifications may be lopsided. For example, when I was a young lawyer, I had a cardiologist on the stand as an expert witness. Wanting to impress the jury, I asked the doctor to tell us something about his medical writing.

Well, he had written a dozen books and 186 monographs, and he was delighted to tell us *all* about them. I couldn't stop him. And the plaintiff's lawyer didn't *want* to stop him because he could anticipate all those juicy questions he was going to ask on cross-examination.

When that time came, it was an easy matter for the lawyer to imply to the jury that the expert witness wasn't a "real" physician—he was a professional author whose time was mainly devoted to writing about what he believed doctors should do.

The moral: If an expert witness has extensive qualifications, suggest to your attorney that he bring out only those that bear on the case at hand. You can help your lawyer with further suggestions on what to emphasize, and what to look out for.

Along with professional writers, beware of "hired guns"—expert witnesses who will work for anyone provided they get paid. It's very easy for a plaintiff's attorney to bring out the fact that these witnesses are mercenaries whose medical opinions are custom-made for sale.

Be careful, too, about picking an expert witness whose career has largely been in medical schools or training centers. I've seen more than a few of these witnesses deflated by a simple comment from the plaintiff's attorney: "But, Doctor, I don't understand. You're supposed to be an expert on this medical subject, but your knowledge seems to come from theory rather than practice. You have no office, no practice in the accepted sense, and you rarely deal with a real patient."

The jury, of course, is left with the impression that this isn't a "real" doctor.

2. *Is the expert able and willing to devote adequate time to preparation for the trial?* If there's any doubt about this, discard the candidate. I've seen too many good cases go down the drain because of expert witnesses who couldn't or wouldn't do proper research, sit in on pretrial consultations, and take part in discovery procedures.

3. *Is the expert familiar with the well-known texts and treatises in his field?* What I'm getting at here is that an expert witness should have professional balance—a physician who practices good medicine and keeps up with the literature in his field. In short, he should be able to handle questions about pertinent medical papers and books.

4. *Is the expert very old or very young?* I don't want to seem discriminatory, but it's an unfortunate fact that some jurors are put off by what I've heard them call "young whippersnappers" or "old duffers." They just don't believe that such doctors are in the best years of their professional lives. So, all things being equal, strive for an experienced expert who's mature, but not too mature.

5. *Are you sure your experts will be paid reasonable fees for court appearances, preparation, and waiting time?* Check with your insurance carrier and make sure *before* the expert enters the case. An expert's professional time is valuable, and he's entitled to get properly paid for it. If he's not, you may end up with a disgruntled witness on the stand—and that can be the worst kind.

Now, let's say *you* are the expert witness. What should you do? What should you not do? The answers are the next order of business.

HOW TO BE AN EFFECTIVE EXPERT WITNESS

VII

First of all, be absolutely frank and impartial in your medical opinions. The fact that one side or another has retained you as an expert witness doesn't mean they want only opinions that will help *their* side. They also want to know about any nasty surprises the opposition may spring.

It's equally important to maintain an air of impartiality on the stand. I once tried a Federal court case in which a surgeon was an expert witness for the plaintiff. Called to rebut portions of evidence I had introduced for the defendant-doctor, the surgeon hurried to the stand, plumped himself down, leaned forward, and emphatically announced, "Yes, I have an opinion."

It was funny in a way, since no one had yet asked him anything. Some of the jurors and spectators actually laughed. It was no laughing matter for the judge. He sternly ordered the witness to wait until a question was put to him and not to make voluntary statements.

The plaintiff's lawyers weren't laughing, either. They knew their overeager witness had made his partisanship only too clear, thus undermining his credibility.

When I questioned the witness, I addressed him pleasantly. "Doctor," I said, "you've obviously been well-prepared for this trial, so—"

"Are you saying I've been coached?" the witness broke in angrily.

"Coached is your word," I responded, "not mine." I then went on to ask a number of medical questions.

Perhaps I looked a bit dubious about the answers, because the surgeon impatiently interrupted me again. "Are you questioning my competence as a doctor?" he demanded. "If you are, let me tell you—"

He then began reeling off a list of his professional accomplishments. The judge finally stopped him.

By then, of course, the witness had revealed himself as a prima donna. Worse, he had committed a cardinal sin on the stand by losing his temper. The jury was left with the impression that they were dealing with a riled-up know-it-all.

A know-it-all attitude can backfire in other situations, especially where two or more conflicting schools of medical thought are involved. In one instance, when I questioned a medical expert about a school of thought he obviously didn't agree with, he flatly declared, "That's bunk!" Jurors will wonder about a mind as closed as that.

Another witness I questioned denounced believers in an opposing school of thought as "a bunch of idiots!" In effect, he was disparaging quite a large portion of the medical profession, and since his own opinions didn't sound too logical, the jurors just may have had some doubts about which school the "idiots" followed.

So if you're testifying on different schools of thought, be prepared to discuss each impartially. If you favor one or the other, explain your point of view without knocking the opposition.

And don't be tough or overbearing when dealing with opposition lawyers or expert witnesses. Some jurors may identify with those lawyers and witnesses, and in effect you'll be getting tough with the jury.

On the other hand, don't undersell yourself, no matter

how modest you may be. One of the most prestigious internists in the country was once testifying as an expert witness for a client of mine. On the stand, he had an unfortunate habit of preceding his answers with such remarks as, "Well, this is just my opinion, you understand, and there are undoubtedly many doctors who would disagree with it, but—"

He sounded uncertain and insecure, and he wasn't nearly as effective as I'd thought he would be.

How far can opposition lawyers go in questioning an expert medical witness? Let's start with qualifications. In many states, in theory, anyone who has a medical license is qualified to express medical opinions in court. In fact, however, if you're a G.P. and you set yourself up as an expert witness on neurological procedures, prepare to have your qualifications torn to shreds by the opposition lawyer. It's not wise to step out of your field.

Beware, too, of the attorney who tries to slip in questions that aren't relevant to your medical qualifications. For example, the lawyer might ask, "How many times have you been divorced?" Don't answer. The attorney for your side will object—such personal prying is *not* allowed.

Unfortunately, in some instances, the witness will respond before the objection is made, thus planting a seed of doubt in the mind of a juror who, say, is strongly opposed to divorce.

You *can* be asked about your own professional preferences in treatment, but you *cannot* specifically be asked what you would have done had you been the defendant-doctor. That's where the hypothetical question comes in. You *can* be asked whether the physician described in a hypothetical case followed usual and customary standards.

Here's the general structure of the hypothetical:

Q. Doctor, assume that in a community of about 75,000 persons, a licensed physician is engaged during the summer of (appropriate year) in practicing as a specialist in the field of (appropriate specialty). Assume further that a patient (appropriate description) comes under the care of that physician and (the experiences of the plaintiff-patient and the actions of the defendant-physician, leading up to the developments claimed to have constituted malpractice).

Now, Doctor, based upon that hypothetical set of facts and your assuming them to be true, have you an opinion, based upon a reasonable degree of medical certainty, as to (the specific opinion to be solicited)?

A. Yes, I have an opinion.

Q. Please state that opinion to the judge and jury.

A. (The expert gives his opinion.)

You can't be called upon to give testimony based on speculation or possibilities, or even probabilities. Your opinion must be related to "a reasonable degree of medical certainty." If that phrase is omitted, the attorney for your side will—or should—object. Wait for the objection. (For more on the "hypothetical question," see Chapter X.)

Along with assisting in the selection of expert medical witnesses, a defendant-doctor can help in picking jurors. I'll explain how in the next chapter.

SELECTING THE RIGHT JURY

VIII

Jury selection is generally considered to be the province of judges and lawyers. I've found, however, that defendant-doctors can often make useful suggestions and help in other ways. More about that later. First, let's look at the process of selecting a jury.

Practices vary between the Federal judiciary and state court systems. But in general, the judge and the attorneys involved will jointly examine the prospective jurors. Those prospects will be provided with sufficient information to acquaint them with the nature of the case at hand, so they will be able to answer questions about their qualifications to sit as jurors. The lawyers on each side, of course, will attempt to pick or eliminate candidates that they feel will or will not be right for their particular purposes.

As the defendant, you'll be sitting at your counsel's table—a good position from which to watch the whole show. That's fine. What may not be so fine is that the jury prospects will be in a good position to watch *you*. And I've had more than a few clients who got off to a bad start by squirming, wiggling, frowning, staring at the ceiling, or even glowering at the jury candidates as though they were the enemy.

I once defended a doctor who hunched forward in his chair, crouched over the table, and endlessly tore sheets of paper into tiny bits. I whispered to him several times to stop, but he kept on doing it. Eventually, I won the case on the evidence, but I always thought the jury candidates must have been unfavorably impressed by the nervous actions of the defendant.

So be calm and composed. Sit comfortably erect in your chair. Look at each candidate as he's questioned, but don't stare belligerently. Make your expression one of interest.

Listen carefully to the questions and answers, and pay attention to the body language. In one case, the defendant-doctor called my attention to the way one candidate would jerk impatiently from side to side when responding to questions about physicians in general.

"He doesn't like doctors," the defendant told me, and I had to agree he was probably right. We managed to keep that fellow off the jury.

You will be allowed to talk to your lawyer during the selection process, but *don't* try to confer while a juror prospect is being questioned. That will distract your lawyer and possibly cause him to miss something important. Wait until there's a break in the questioning, then say what you have to say in a low voice.

Incidentally, it's not wise to huddle continually with your lawyer in the courtroom. That might create an air of conspiracy. So might a lot of note-passing between you. Save your communication for matters of relevance.

What your attorney will particularly want to know is your impression of each candidate. By the very nature of medical practice, most doctors are excellent judges of human nature and behavior. Several examples from my own experience:

○ In one case, a jury candidate remarked that he'd been waiting in court a long while before being called, then added wryly, "I suppose that's the doctor's waiting-room syndrome."

After the questioning, the doctor whispered to me, "I think you'd better skip this one. He sounds like he's had some bad experiences in medical waiting rooms." I skipped him.

○ Another candidate, asked if he'd have any compunction about returning a large verdict against doctors, replied, "No—they can afford it."

Neither my client nor I hesitated in skipping that one, too—for obvious reasons.

○ One particularly breezy prospect was asked if he was familiar with physicians. "Sure," he responded, "I see them around my golf course all the time."

My client had never been on a golf course in his life, but he turned thumbs down on that candidate.

Don't look only for flaws in the prospect. Try to spot candidates who appear to be intelligent and impartial. Those will be the ones you and your lawyer will particularly want to reach during the trial.

Don't expect your lawyer to accept all of your suggestions. He respects your opinion, but remember that he's there to represent you with his best professional judgment. Rely on that. Don't argue with him, or sulk. The courtroom is a goldfish bowl, and you're right in the center of it, under close observation by people who may be swayed adversely by your performance at the counsel's table as well as in the witness box.

Keep that in mind not only during the jury selection, but in subsequent proceedings.

During opening statements, for example, you'll probably hear the opposition lawyer make highly critical remarks about you. It's instinctive to look upset, outraged, or even hostile. Don't give in to that instinct. The lawyer is just doing his job. Look at him attentively and objectively, not with hostility.

Likewise, when your attorney is making his opening statement or closing argument, don't nod your head or make any other expression of approval. I once defended an elderly country doctor who was a likeable old fellow, if somewhat uninhibited in his ways. When I made a particularly significant point in my opening statement, my client slapped his knee and chortled, "That's tellin' 'em, Jack! Give it to 'em!"

A lot of judges would have thrown us out of court or read the riot act to us, but this one was laughing too hard. He just admonished the doctor.

Another hint: Your attorney may be widely experienced in medico-legal matters, but every case is different. Discuss with him what he's going to include in his opening statement. There just may be something in there that isn't accurate or can't be proved. If not caught in the beginning, it can backfire later and blow your defense apart.

Similarly, when your attorney is preparing his closing argument, it's advisable to go over with him the principal points brought up during the trial, especially those involving medical technicalities. That advance session can be helpful.

It's also helpful for medical witnesses to know how to make a good first impression when ready to take the stand. We'll go into that next.

IX

WILL THE WAY YOU COME ON TURN THEM OFF?

You may be an expert in your own field, but you can still be a flop as a medical witness if you make an unfavorable impression en route to the stand—or on it. Many times I've seen medical witnesses look bad in court before they even started to testify. The doctor who dashes into the courtroom late is a particularly obvious offender; he's bound to irritate the judge and jury. Sometimes the doctor who comes in too early doesn't project a very good image, either.

I remember one specialist who showed up in court at 10 in the morning, even though he wasn't due to testify until 3:30 that afternoon. He sat slouched in a back seat, filing his fingernails. One juror later said to me: "I was surprised when he got up to testify. The way he was lolling around there, I thought he was just another courtroom bum." A second juror added, "I figured he couldn't have been much in demand as a doctor if he had enough free time to sit there in court all day."

Of course, this doesn't mean that the medical witness should wait until the last minute before putting in an appearance. I encourage my medical witnesses to get into the courtroom about half an hour before they're due to testify. If they can manage it, this allows them time to acquire a feeling for what's going on. It also permits me to confer with them, if necessary, before they take the stand.

However, I don't encourage a medical witness to make an entrance in the grand manner. I still shudder when I think of a rather overpowering surgeon who barged into court, stomped down the aisle, and bellowed to me while I was examining another witness on the stand: "Horsley, I'm here! Where do you want me to sit?" Even though the surgeon later testified competently, this didn't quite compensate for his initial impression on the judge and jury—which was, to put it mildly, shattering.

That first impression is so important that the medical witness should have it in mind when he arrives at the courthouse. If he's been told not to go into the courtroom until called—which happens occasionally in civil cases—he should give his name to the bailiff at the door. Then he should stay away from the door. I've known of doctors who were disqualified as medical witnesses because they were suspected of eavesdropping at the courtroom entrance.

In most instances, the medical witness will go directly into the courtroom. He should walk in quietly. If there's a section reserved for witnesses, the bailiff will direct him to it. If not, he can take the most convenient seat. He shouldn't try to speak to the attorney who requested his appearance. If he has any last-minute information for the attorney, he should write a note and hand it to the bailiff for delivery.

Now, there's something about the spectator's section of a courtroom that's conducive to chumminess. I suppose it's the feeling that one is watching a drama unfold. And, as in a theater, the spectator is sometimes impelled to comment on the proceedings—often as not, to a perfect stranger who just happens to be sitting next to him.

One medical witness I know was sitting alongside just such a stranger during a trial not long ago. They struck up a conversation and talked about various aspects of the case. Later, when it developed that the "stranger" was another witness, both were disqualified. In another case, a mistrial was declared after a medical witness got into a courtroom conversation with a man who turned out to be a prospective juror. In short, if you're a medical witness waiting to be called to the stand, don't discuss the case with anyone near you.

WILL THE WAY YOU COME ON TURN THEM OFF?

The call to the stand, when it comes, creates a crisis of sorts for many doctors—even veterans at testifying. At the very moment when they should be at their best—the moment they first come under the scrutiny of judge and jury—they often appear at their worst. Some hang their heads and shuffle up to the stand furtively, as though they were afraid or had something to hide. Others—and these are by far the greatest offenders—gallop toward the stand and literally take the oath on the run. The jury is left with the impression that the witness doesn't really take the oath seriously and is mainly concerned with getting the whole thing over with in a hurry.

It's best to approach the stand at a pace that's neither fast nor slow. To ward off stage fright, keep your eyes on the clerk who's waiting to administer the oath. At this point, an occasional doctor falls into another trap. He'll raise his right hand halfheartedly and mumble the response to the oath. Commenting on a medical witness who'd done this, a juror once told me, "He was so sloppy, I figured he'd be sloppy in his practice, too."

The correct procedure is to stand directly in front of the clerk and—in most courts—place your left hand on the Bible. Hold your right hand high with the fingers straight, and continue to look at the clerk while he swears you in. When he finishes reciting the oath, say "I do" in a clear voice that can be heard by everyone in the courtroom. Then take the stand.

Now comes another critical moment. Perhaps discomfited at becoming the focus of the jury's gaze, one medical witness will fidget and fuss when he sits down in the witness chair. Another may slump onto the base of his spine and cross his legs. As noted earlier, this invariably leads to such nervous mannerisms as recrossing the legs, pulling at an earlobe, massaging the chin, and moving a hand over the mouth. It's really more comfortable, and certainly less likely to convey an image of uneasiness, to sit up straight in the witness chair, with both feet set firmly on the floor and hands lightly clasped in your lap.

The judge and jury will size you up in other ways that have nothing to do with your competence as a medical witness. Such externals as your dress, your voice, and your manner may seem trivial, but they often influence jury decisions.

Let's take the manner of dress first. Clothes may not make the man, but they can certainly undo the medical witness. I've seen doctors take the stand in everything from gaudy sports shirts to hospital whites complete with stethoscope dangling from the neck. Some have shown up in bedroom slippers. One big-city specialist arrived at a rural courtroom sporting a neckerchief and monocle. He came close to being laughed right out of court.

I don't mean that the medical witness must necessarily wear a somber, subdued suit. In these days of liberated male fashions, it's permissible to show some color and style. It's not advisable, however, to appear on the witness stand in anything that's likely to distract the jury. If you have a choice between a plain blue suit and a fancy plaid outfit with wide lapels and flared trouser-bottoms, choose the blue. Jurors might admire the plaid number, but they might also pay less heed to what you're saying.

The same applies to accessories. I was once present in court when an internist took the stand in a neat, conservative gray suit. The moment he sat down, though, he crossed his legs and displayed a pair of the brightest scarlet socks I've ever seen. What's more, he kept re-crossing his legs all through his testimony. The socks flashed back and forth like a couple of playful redbirds. The jurors, I noticed, were so fascinated by those socks that they concentrated more on the doctor's ankles than on his words.

WILL THE WAY YOU COME ON TURN THEM OFF?

One last note about clothes: Make sure they're comfortable. A medical witness who keeps tugging at an overly snug collar, or shifting in the witness chair to compensate for tight trousers, looks uneasy. The jury just might get uneasy, too—and unfriendly.

Another way to irritate the jurors is to speak so softly that they have trouble hearing you. In advising medical witnesses on how to keep the voice up, I tell them to project it to the farthest juror.

That doesn't mean the witness should shout. I know a surgeon who makes an excellent expert medical witness except for the roar of his voice, which sounds like an express train coming out of a tunnel.

When he was due to testify in one case, I was in another courtroom with a colleague. We'd just finished a court session, and I suggested we go and listen to the surgeon testify. "Why move?" said my colleague. "We can hear him from here."

That surgeon, I might add, isn't often called as an expert witness. His "hog-calling" voice, as he himself has termed it, greatly diminishes the effectiveness of his testimony.

A speech impediment may also detract from a witness's testimony, but not always. I once defended a pathologist who stuttered. When I put him on the stand, I was a bit apprehensive. The apprehension grew as he labored to bring out his words.

Then I happened to glance at the jury. All were listening intently, and I saw empathy in their faces. They were "with" that witness—they could see he was striving hard to overcome a speech affliction that was congenital and largely beyond his control. Consequently, the jurors listened carefully so they could extract every bit of information that the witness was trying to provide them.

He won that case on its merits. The stuttering, which I had feared would be a liability, turned out to be an asset.

The pace of speech is also important. Some witnesses feel they have to get everything out in a rush. This makes it difficult for jurors to understand what's going on. It also puts pressure on the court reporter, possibly causing him to leave gaps in testimony.

Glance occasionally at the reporter. He usually sits at a table in front of the witness stand. If he appears rushed or hurried, slow the speed of your voice.

Even if the medical witness speaks clearly, dresses neatly, and sits up straight, he can still destroy it all with a bad demeanor. In extreme instances, I've seen doctor-witnesses grin at the spectators, scowl at the jury, or look at the opposition lawyer with obvious hate or scorn.

Some mannerisms of speech can also be annoying. I've questioned many witnesses who tried to fill in gaps in their testimony by saying "Well, you know—" The jurors *don't* know. The witness is there to tell them.

Beware, too, of distracting habits, such as fiddling with a necktie, tugging at an ear, or scratching the head and other parts of the body.

I once had a witness who habitually placed a hand on his chin and extended the index finger across his mouth. The opposition lawyer finally asked the judge to direct the witness to remove the finger from his mouth so the jury could understand what he was saying.

That sort of interruption can not only be embarrassing to a witness, it can be damaging to his testimony. In pretrial conferences, it's wise for a witness to ask the lawyer on his side if he's noticed any potentially harmful habits, gestures, or facial expressions. Sometimes, as I've learned to do, the lawyer will voluntarily make suggestions. It's advisable to follow them.

WILL THE WAY YOU COME ON TURN THEM OFF?

The best witness gives an impression of relaxed but serious candor. He doesn't divide his attention among the spectators, the judge, and the jury, but devotes it fully to the lawyer who is about to probe his qualifications—still another critical moment.

Physicians, of course, vary greatly in their backgrounds and credentials. They also vary greatly in the size of their egos. Some want to say too little about themselves; others try to say too much. In a Kentucky case, for example, a medical witness testified that he was qualified to practice in Florida, Kentucky, Ohio, Michigan, Illinois, and Indiana. Largely as a result of his testimony, damages of $20,000 were awarded to each of several victims of an automobile accident. After the trial, however, it was proved that the witness was licensed to practice only in Kentucky. The judgment in the case was then set aside and a new trial was ordered.

Any medical witness who's tempted to build himself up falsely might well keep in mind an admonition of the American Medical Association: "Don't exaggerate. Any attempt to puff up your qualifications . . . is apt to be exposed, to your embarrassment."

Nonetheless, false modesty is no virtue in a medical witness. He shouldn't hold back from revealing anything outstanding in his schooling, training, experience, and professional achievements. Mention of any specialty board certification is a must. So are hospital affiliations, and any offices held in medical societies. Honors, prizes, or awards also add to the authority of the witness.

If broken bones are at issue in the case, a jury anywhere is naturally going to give weight to the testimony of a doctor with expertise and experience in that field. Still more weight can be added by taking into consideration the sort of people living in the area. In a highly industrialized Midwest city several years ago, I brought out that the doctor on the stand did part-time work for an industrial union. In another case that was tried in a college town, I emphasized the fact that a medical witness was active in scientific research. The aim is to get the jury to identify as closely as possible with the witness.

That may sound crafty, but it's simply a means of establishing rapport between the jury and the medical witness—the same sort of rapport that all good doctors try to create between themselves and their patients. The trouble is that a medical man may not be the best judge of which qualifications will mean the most to a jury. That's why discussion of this subject is essential in pretrial conferences between doctor and lawyer.

Some doctors want to detail everything they've ever accomplished, right down to that college chess championship. That's the worst thing they can do. If it doesn't bore the jurors, it will annoy them as a display of egotism. The best course is to decide on a select list with the lawyer, then let him bring out the qualifications in court through a series of crisp, to-the-point questions. Thus, the authority of the witness is clearly drawn, and the stage is set for the next step in the trial—direct examination. We deal with that next.

DIRECT EXAMINATION SHOULD BE A BREEZE

X

Direct examination puts the medical witness in a particularly favorable position. He's like a baseball player at batting practice. He faces not an opposition pitcher but a member of his own team—in this instance, the lawyer with whom he's working. The pitches come over the plate nice and easy. Yet very often, instead of taking advantage of the situation and hitting a home run, the medical witness strikes out.

Why? One reason is a fault that leads to errors in court as well as on the baseball field—overeagerness. Here's an example: In a West Coast case that I observed, an eminent orthopedist was giving testimony for the plaintiff in a personal injury suit. He was well dressed and articulate, and he had done his homework for the trial. Nevertheless, as I watched the faces of the jurors, I could see they were having doubts about the witness—and I could understand why. In his eagerness to show his stuff, he was responding too quickly to questions. Sometimes the lawyer wouldn't even have a question completed before the doctor leaped in with an answer. It was like a slickly rehearsed act—and jurors are notoriously suspicious of anyone who appears to be acting on the witness stand.

So are opposition lawyers. In this same case, when the orthopedist came under cross-examination, the opposing attorney started off congratulating the doctor on his testimony during direct examination. Then came the needle. "Obviously," said the lawyer, "you've had some good coaching." An objection was made, but not before the jury had got the point.

That orthopedist, I'd like to emphasize, was no newcomer to courtrooms. He'd appeared in a number of cases. Yet he'd never learned the cardinal rule in testifying during direct examination: Take your time when answering questions. Even though you've previously gone over this ground with the lawyer for your side, listen carefully to his questions and weigh your answers. That adds to the convincingness of your testimony.

On the other hand, of course, the medical witness shouldn't take too much time in answering questions. The jury might then get the idea that he's doubtful or reluctant. Dickens, who knew his courts, summed it all up when he wrote: "Lawyers hold that there are two kinds of particularly bad witnesses: a reluctant witness, and a too willing witness."

The too willing witness is especially liable to run into trouble when he volunteers information. Example: In a Southern case, a G.P. was testifying for a woman who claimed damages for injuries allegedly received when a tinned-goods display in a supermarket toppled onto her. On direct examination, he was asked how long he'd treated her for those injuries. "Two months," he said.

That was enough. That was all he'd been asked. Yet he added: "Of course, a couple of years ago, she was also under my care for about six months."

The woman's lawyer quickly cut the doctor off, but now a door had been opened for the opposition lawyer. On cross-examination, he immediately began to delve into the reason for the woman's previous treatment by

DIRECT EXAMINATION SHOULD BE A BREEZE

the medical witness. Although it was an ailment dissimilar to the injuries she said she'd suffered in the supermarket, a doubt was created in the minds of the jurors. The woman won her case, but the amount of damages awarded was small.

The moral for the medical witness: Be brief and to the point on direct examination. Your answers should cover only what the questions call for. To offer more may open a Pandora's box filled with nasty surprises.

That goes double when the information volunteered concerns insurance. Some time ago, I was present in a court where the owner of a taxi company was being sued for damages in a personal injury case. A medical witness, giving testimony for the plaintiff, casually remarked that he'd heard the taxi owner was "covered with plenty of insurance." This promptly brought down the wrath of the judge and caused a mistrial.

Even when the consequences aren't that drastic, slips such as those create the impression that the medical witness is generally careless about what he says. This is true even in relatively minor matters, such as happened once when I was questioning an internist during direct examination. He was a good witness, except for one thing: Whenever I asked him about certain dimensions that were pertinent to the case, he'd hold up his hands and say, "About this wide," or, "About so high."

I explained repeatedly that specific answers were needed for the court record, but he persisted in this unthinking mannerism. It eventually sparked a rebuke from the judge. The jurors, I could see, were also very much annoyed by his actions.

There are other ways in which sloppy mannerisms of speech can weaken the testimony of a medical witness during direct examination. Probably the worst offender is the doctor who qualifies his remarks with such terms as, "it would seem," "indications are," "possibly," "perhaps," or, "I suppose." Many doctors are conservative by nature, but on the witness stand it's best to be as specific as possible. Otherwise, the jury gets the feeling that the witness isn't very sure of himself.

The jury may also wonder about the medical witness who sprinkles his testimony with such phrases as, "I honestly believe," and, "to tell the truth." It's taken for granted that the witness is on the stand to be honest and to tell the truth. Rather than enhancing credibility, emphasizing those points creates suspicion.

The best way to strengthen your testimony is to use graphic, precise terms. Pain, for example, is a very general word. It could mean anything from a headache to a throbbing toe. Whenever possible, state the area of the pain and describe it: stabbing, dull, intermittent, constant, or whatever it may be.

Most doctors know by now that they should avoid technical or scientific terms on the witness stand, or if their use is unavoidable, to explain them in plain English. In short, the doctor should define each medical term as he uses it, without being didactic.

For example: "The patient had a comminuted fracture in the upper third of the right femur. That means he suffered a crushing break in the thigh bone near the top of the thigh. Instead of a clean break, it left small splinters of bone around the place where the leg was broken."

Sometimes a medical witness will make an unfortunate choice of words, even in plain English. I came across a rather startling example of that several years ago, when I was researching a case involving a spinal injury. In one of the cases I read about, a radiologist on the witness stand had described the cervical spine of the plaintiff as normal, but with a little "lipping." Damages of $400 were awarded.

In another, almost identical case, the radiologist-witness described the cervical spine as normal, but with a

DIRECT EXAMINATION SHOULD BE A BREEZE

little "spiking." The plaintiff in that one was awarded damages of $30,000—a figure that was way out of line. The jury, it developed, had voted for the high award because they'd imagined that "spikes" were growing out of the plaintiff's backbone. The lesson is obvious: In choosing a nontechnical term to describe a medical condition, be sure it isn't going to mislead the jury.

Be sure, too, that you don't fall into the trap of trying to "help" the lawyer directly examining you. That situation usually develops when the doctor on the stand feels the medical aspects of the case aren't being presented properly. I was in court once when a surgeon repeatedly interrupted the attorney with such remarks as, "I think what you're trying to bring out, Counselor, is—" and "If I may put that another way—." The exasperated lawyer finally had to tell his own witness just to answer the questions as they were put to him.

I spoke to the surgeon after the trial was over, and he seemed genuinely surprised that the lawyer had jumped on him that way. "I was only trying to help the guy," he explained.

Fine. We trial lawyers need all the help we can get, but not in the form of leading remarks from our own witnesses on the stand. That kind of "help" puts the witness in a particularly bad light in the eyes of the jurors; it makes him appear partisan.

In short, the medical witness must maintain professional objectivity. If a friendly lawyer asks a question that's badly phrased, simply say, "Would you please clarify the question?" If he doesn't provide enough information in a question, request additional details. If you still don't understand the question, say so. The worst thing you can do is to guess at an answer.

One important clarification: Although you shouldn't try to guide the examiner in his questioning, you should correct him if he makes a remark that isn't completely right. If you don't put him straight, the opposition lawyer probably will. Here's how one veteran medical witness politely but firmly handled a situation of this sort:

During the trial of Albert DeSalvo, "The Boston Strangler," psychiatrist James A. Brussel was testifying for the defense. Questioning him on direct examination was the celebrated lawyer, F. Lee Bailey, who asked at one point: "Isn't the DeSalvo record at Bridgewater (mental institution) consistent with your diagnosis of paranoia?" The psychiatrist responded with scrupulous honesty: "In some places, yes. In other places, no." The lawyer then asked, "Now, is neurosis a less severe form of psychoneurosis?" Brussel promptly corrected him: "No. It's a shortened form of the word."

I've sometimes noticed that a medical witness will be startled or become upset on the stand when the opposition lawyer makes an objection. Those objections shouldn't be taken personally, even if the judge sustains the motion and instructs the jury to disregard what's been said. It simply means that the witness testified to something that wasn't legally proper.

Very often on direct examination the expert medical witness will be asked to give an opinion based on a series of assumptions. That's known as the hypothetical question, although it's not all that hypothetical, as we learned in Chapter VII. It must conform to facts that are substantiated—or will be substantiated—in the evidence of the case. Thus, if a patient's jaw showed no swelling on January 1, a hypothetical question cannot be framed to assume swelling on that date.

Even experienced medical witnesses are sometimes tripped by the hypothetical question. Admittedly, it's a clumsy legal device, and to some doctors a roundabout way of doing things. Nevertheless, it's necessary. Let's say the medical witness examined the victim of a car crash quite some time after the accident. The doctor has only the patient's word for what happened, which is hearsay and not admissible in court.

DIRECT EXAMINATION SHOULD BE A BREEZE

To get around this legal obstacle, the crash victim testifies in court as to what happened and how it affected him. When the expert medical witness takes the stand, the victim's lawyer puts to him a hypothetical question created from the facts of the case.

Trouble arises at this point if the hypothetical question hasn't been worked out in advance by the lawyer and his expert medical witness. The question should contain nothing that's not absolutely necessary to form a medical opinion. Yet, time and time again, I've heard lawyers start their hypothetical questions like this: "Doctor, assume as true the following: A 42-year-old steel worker is driving his car down a straight stretch of highway. He's on his side of the road, and he's driving well within the speed limit of 60 miles an hour. He has consumed no alcoholic beverages, nor has he taken any drugs. Suddenly he's overtaken by another car, which forces him off the road, resulting in a severe crash."

The lawyer finally gets to the medical details, but not before the jury is well aware that he's loaded the hypothetical question with arguments for his side. The opposition lawyer is well aware of this, too.

On cross-examination of the expert medical witness, he's going to have a field day, making such sarcastic remarks as, "I was impressed, Doctor, by the skillful manner in which you can form a medical opinion from the assumption that a man is driving on his own side of the road."

The doctor is thus linked with his lawyer in an implied conspiracy to influence the jury unfairly. To avoid that implication, an expert medical witness should (1) insist on a pretrial conference with the lawyer, and (2) find out the points that are to go into the framing of the hypothetical question. The doctor should firmly resist any attempt by the lawyer to omit any pertinent medical details, or to load the question with nonmedical irrelevancies. In this way, the doctor can save himself from unnecessary trouble on the stand.

Trouble can be avoided, too, if the doctor comes to court with properly prepared medical records. We'll go into that aspect of testifying in the next chapter.

HOW CARELESS RECORDS CAN MESS YOU UP

XI

The witness, an internist, was testifying in a personal injury case. The plaintiff had been his patient for more than a decade. When asked about certain treatment he'd given two years earlier, the internist requested permission to consult his records. This was granted; the witness glanced through the charts, and responded to the question. Before he could put his records away, however, the opposition lawyer asked to examine them. This exchange took place:

Q. "Have all the entries in these records been made by you, Doctor?"

A. "They have."

Q. "You call the plaintiff Joe?"

A. "Yes. We've known each other a long time."

Q. "Then I take it you were referring to the plaintiff when you made this entry: 'A lot of Joe's trouble stems from his wife. She's a bitch on wheels.' "

That internist nearly collapsed with embarrassment. Most doctors are more discreet in recording details about a patient, yet it's surprising how many physicians put irrelevant, but potentially dangerous comments on the record. Here are a few of the many I've heard read out in court over the years: "She's too fat and flabby." "It's all in his mind." "This fellow has owed me $300 for more than a year." "What this woman really needs is a good bath."

When a medical witness uses his records to refresh his memory on the stand, they become part of the evidence. The opposition lawyer can examine them, comment on them, or read from them. When making entries on patient records, therefore, it's wise not to put down anything you wouldn't want read in court.

Indiscreet comments aren't, of course, the only way in which records can make trouble for doctors on the witness stand. Some time ago, I read an excellent editorial in the bulletin of the Westchester (N.Y.) County Medical Society entitled "The Medical Records Mess." The writer particularly deplored: "Dog-eared cards. Huge folders stuffed with multipurpose slips of paper. Illegible handwriting. Hieroglyphic abbreviations without a Rosetta Stone. Old hospital summaries mixed with current progress notes. Nine ECG mounts to the inch. The medical auditor is first irritated, then frustrated, and, eventually, despairing."

Well, many a lawyer has also been irritated and frustrated by doctors who keep messy records. A number of years ago I put the defendant in a malpractice case on the stand to testify for himself. He was a personable physician and quite articulate. The testimony progressed smoothly until he had to resort to his records to refresh his memory.

I groaned inwardly when I saw the records. They were on smudged, creased, 2 × 4-inch file cards. Worse, the doctor couldn't find what he was looking for. As he shuffled the tiny cards back and forth, it became obvious that they hadn't been kept in order. He even dropped a couple of the cards on the floor.

The physician lost the case. I was disappointed, but not wholly surprised. Juries tend to figure that if a doctor is careless about his records, he's probably careless in other ways, too.

HOW CARELESS RECORDS CAN MESS YOU UP

Although many doctors have their patient records typed up, my experiences in court indicate that a majority still write them out in longhand. This creates another problem: illegible handwriting. I've repeatedly observed medical witnesses stumbling and stammering because they had trouble figuring out the substance of their records. I've even seen a few who had to give up and admit they couldn't read their own writing.

Whether or not you have *that* difficulty, it's advisable to go over any pertinent records just before appearing in court. That often eliminates the need to refer to them on the stand—which can be an awkward process that slows up the trial. And juries are inclined to get restless or bored when proceedings drag.

On the other hand, juries get highly suspicious when they hear that the records of a medical witness have been altered. That doesn't happen very often, but when it does, it can be catastrophic for the testifying doctor. In an East Coast case, for instance, a G.P. was charged with malpractice after a middle-aged executive died from penicillin reaction. The patient's family contended that the G.P. had administered penicillin without asking the patient if he was allergic to it. On the stand, the defendant-doctor insisted the patient had told him he had no allergies.

In going over his records, however, the G.P. noticed he hadn't made any entry about the inquiry into the patient's allergies. Without checking with his lawyer, he wrote into the record, "Patient said he had no allergies." The insertion was squeezed in, and made in a shade of ink different from that of the original entry. The alteration was obvious, and the opposition lawyer quickly spotted it. The G.P. was forced to admit on the stand that he had changed the record. Not only did he lose the case, his reputation was so badly tarnished that he had to give up his private practice and take an administrative post in another city.

What that G.P. should have done was to write in the additional information, and date and initial it. Then, when he took the stand, he should have explained the alteration before his records were introduced. That's the only way he could have avoided the implication that he was trying to cover up vital evidence.

A doctor should also initial entries in patient records that have not been made by him. Failure to do so can lead to complications on the witness stand, as an internist I know found out. He was testifying in an injury case when the cross-examiner said: "Doctor, I notice there are entries in the patient's record in handwriting other than yours. Who made those entries?"

"My nurse. They pertain to services she performed, such as taking the height and weight, and giving injections."

"In other words, Doctor, if you were to testify about this patient's weight, that would be hearsay. You cannot testify for your nurse."

"But she performed those services at my request and under my supervision."

"There's nothing in the record to indicate that."

The lawyer then made a motion that the internist be restricted in his testimony to what he himself had put into the record. The motion was upheld, and the medical witness was considerably hampered during his session on the stand—a difficulty he could have avoided simply by initialing the entries made by the nurse. That would have verified his statement that she had performed certain services at his request and under his supervision.

Another point in this regard: The findings of a radiologist should be entered in a patient's records only after the treating or examining physician has reviewed the films and confirmed the report. That enables the physician to testify in court about his own interpretation of the X-ray photographs.

If the medical witness is the plaintiff's physician, he should take the patient's records with him to court. If not, he should ask the lawyer concerned if any records will be needed. Some jurisdictions allow photostats of records to be used; others don't. In general, it's best to take along the originals.

What should good records contain? Here's a checklist:

Dates. Most doctors are conscientious about recording the dates of office visits, but many slip up on dating such things as telephone calls, lab reports, and consultations. All pertinent dates should be entered in the record.

Source of the patient visit. Note the circumstances that brought the patient to you. If he's not one of your regular patients and a lawyer sent him, that definitely should be written down.

Nature of the complaint. If an accident is involved, have the patient explain the how, when, and where of it—preferably with your tape recorder in action. In writing the medical history, try to use the patient's own words.

Results of the examination. The doctor should carefully separate his own findings from what the patient told him. For example, if the word "anxiety" appears, the doctor should explain whether he found the patient to be suffering from anxiety, or whether the patient himself used the word. If scars or bruises are present, their size and location should be specified. And, of course, the patient's height, weight, blood pressure, and pulse should be recorded.

Diagnosis. If there's any uncertainty about this, it should be marked "provisional." Also note diagnostic aids used, such as lab tests, X-rays, and consultations.

Treatment. Write down the type, along with details of each step of treatment.

Prognosis. This should include the extent of disability—whether the patient is able to work at his job, and whether he'll be handicapped in the future.

Financial data. Although this doesn't have to be written into the clinical record, it should be attached to the record when taken to court. List the bills sent and fees received, including all dates, and a note about who actually paid the fees.

Along with clinical and financial records, a medical witness is entitled to refresh his memory from an appointment schedule, a diary, an insurance report, an account book, or a memo. Care should be exercised, however, in the way such documents are used. Consider what happened at the trial of Lieut. William L. Calley Jr., when he was charged with murdering civilians in Vietnam. A psychiatrist testifying for the defense asked permission to consult his "notes." When he took the "notes" from his briefcase, the prosecutor asked to see them. They weren't "notes" at all, but an 1,800-word preface to a hypothetical question that the defense lawyer had read to the medical witness on direct examination. The material had not come from the psychiatrist's own findings on Calley, but from an Army sanity board that had examined him.

Both the judge and the prosecutor attacked the medical witness for the misuse of what he had termed his "notes." The psychiatrist then withdrew from the case, and his testimony was stricken from the record. The point is, when you take any paper to the stand with you, be sure you define it correctly if you use it to refresh your memory.

Similarly, if you plan to put on any demonstrations or exhibits during your testimony, be sure to use the most effective techniques. You can read all about those in the following chapter.

BACK UP YOUR WORDS WITH ILLUSTRATIONS

XII

Exhibits and demonstrations can enhance the testimony of a medical witness, provided the presentation is good. The objective is to dramatize a situation that might otherwise seem vague, unclear, or even confusing, to the jury. A particularly dramatic example of this technique was used in a New York case some years ago, in which a chorus girl claimed she'd been raped in the back seat of a taxi. A doctor testifying for the defense said he didn't think the alleged assault had taken place. The jury seemed unconvinced.

The attorney for the defense then had the body of a taxi assembled in the courtroom. Pointing out the leggy proportions of the lady involved and the cramped conditions of the back seat, he contended that rape in the taxi was impossible. That the jury could believe, and the verdict favored the defendant.

Few medical witnesses would be inclined to haul a taxi into court to back up their testimony, but there are many visual means through which doctors on the stand can add weight to their words. Most of these exhibits or demonstrations are quite easy to set up. They let the medical witness indulge in a bit of legitimate showmanship. And juries, I've found, are inclined to be more impressed by evidence they can actually see than by what they just hear about.

For example, I once defended an anesthesiologist who'd been sued for malpractice. The plaintiff claimed that the doctor had bungled a Pentothal anesthetic procedure. Most jury members have little or no knowledge of such matters. Some might well imagine a complicated frightening process.

To clear up such confusion, I had the anesthesiologist demonstrate the procedure. The jury saw that it was simple, and that the claim of the plaintiff was exaggerated. The anesthesiologist had missed a vein in the back of the hand while making the insertion, but no real injury had resulted. The jury's verdict: not guilty.

Another case in which visual evidence was an essential part of the defense involved a Southern surgeon. The plaintiff, on whom he'd operated for the removal of her gallbladder, later complained to him of an ache in the vicinity of the operation. Examination disclosed a nodule in the scar. In a simple office procedure, the surgeon excised the nodule, which was about the size of the end of a man's finger. From this, a suture was removed—the reason for the irritation.

In the petition filed against the surgeon, it was asserted that "a piece of sponge" had been left "in the general vicinity of the abdomen . . ." To clarify this issue, the defendant exhibited in court the types of surgical sponges used during the gallbladder operation. The jury could see that, rather than being of the bathroom variety, they looked like washcloths and towels. The smallest was 4 by 4 inches square—far larger than the suture that had been removed during the office procedure. Clearly impressed by this display, the jury returned a verdict in the surgeon's favor.

The most common exhibit used by medical witnesses is the X-ray photograph. Yet many misuse it. I recall an orthopedist who was testifying in a personal injury case. He was a veteran on the witness stand, but perhaps he'd become a bit bored with court routine. Anyway, when he was asked to examine an X-ray file, he barely glanced at it before stating that no pathology showed. During cross-examination, the opposition lawyer was quick to play up the cursory manner in which the orthopedist had examined the film. The witness, of course, might have seen that film many times before, but all the jurors knew was that he hadn't appeared to be making a conscientious effort to examine it.

BACK UP YOUR WORDS WITH ILLUSTRATIONS

Two other points about X-rays: When a medical witness is handed a film for interpretation, he should identify it for the record with such language as, "I am now viewing an X-ray of the right foot marked Plaintiff's Exhibit C." If the witness is a radiologist, he'd be wise not to go beyond his specialty. The lawyer questioning him may, for example, try to draw him out on the general prognosis. If the radiologist isn't familiar with the patient's complete medical history, it's usually best for him to say he has not formed any opinions, since such questions are out of his field.

Other frequently used medical exhibits are graphs, charts, diagrams, and ordinary photographs. Some doctors are adept at illustrating their testimony with blackboard drawings. The best of these witnesses, in my observation, vary the colors of the chalk used. Multicolored illustrations seem to attract greater jury interest than those in the usual white. One note of caution: If you can't draw fairly well, don't try to use a blackboard in court. Juries become annoyed when an inept drawing confuses rather than clarifies testimony.

Professional artists often provide custom-made drawings for use as medical exhibits. Ted Bloodhart, a California artist who specializes in medical and medico-legal illustration, was commissioned in the case of a woman suing a surgeon for malpractice. Forceps, she said, had been left in her abdomen after surgery. There was no doubt about it: X-rays revealed the forceps.

X-ray films, however, are not very impressive to the untrained eye of the average juror, and the plaintiff's attorney wasn't sure that she would get as large an award as he wanted. So the lawyer had Bloodhart work with an expert medical witness to produce an illustration in natural color of a life-sized human torso. This was cut away to show first a normal, healthy abdomen, then one ravaged by scars and adhesions such as the woman had suffered. The jury decreed a sizable award.

One of the most elaborate demonstrations ever arranged in a medical malpractice case was set up by the noted Ohio defense attorney, R. Crawford Morris. The facts of the case were as follows: A woman had been rushed to a hospital emergency room after a bad car crash. X-rays were taken; they showed two ribs fractured at the junction of the spine and a possible chip fracture.

Six months later, the woman gave premature birth to a daughter who was mentally retarded. The woman then filed a malpractice suit against the hospital's radiology chief, charging negligence. She claimed she had warned the radiologist that she was pregnant; he said she had not.

When the trial opened, the woman was rolled into the courtroom in a wheelchair. She was wearing a straitjacket and crash helmet. Such extreme measures were necessary, her attorney pointedly explained to the jury, because she might otherwise bite herself and bang her head against the wall. (The statute of limitations prevented the woman from bringing a negligence suit for her own condition. But medical witnesses testified during the trial that her condition was proximately caused by the alleged malpractice of the radiologist.)

In the attorney's efforts to establish the seriousness of radiation damage, he pointed out that a woman exposed to from one to 10 roentgens in Denmark may legally get an abortion; if the exposure is more than 10 roentgens, the state recommends abortion.

BACK UP YOUR WORDS WITH ILLUSTRATIONS

Attorney Morris based his defense on a "phantom woman," a $5,000 model built of materials that absorb X-rays as human tissue does. A qualified physicist made tests that showed only 93/100ths of a roentgen had been administered to the plaintiff. Additional scientific testimony indicated that brain damage in the prematurely born child could have been caused by factors other than radiation. The jury needed only 35 minutes to return a verdict in favor of the radiologist.

Juries, I've found, are fascinated by exhibits and demonstrations that show the functions of the human body. Colored plastic torsos, artificial limbs, skeletons, and models of the various parts of the anatomy are highly effective, especially if they contain moving parts.

I remember a case in which a surgeon was accused of malpractice after a knee operation. The patient, a college boy who'd been injured in a football game, claimed the operation had left him with a stiff leg. The surgeon testified that he'd warned the boy of the possibility of such stiffness. Then with a plastic model of a leg and thigh that moved at the knee, he demonstrated exactly how the operation had affected the knee joint and why stiffness had resulted. The jury found for the surgeon.

In the case of a woman who claimed damages for an eye injury suffered in a car crash, an ophthalmologist was called as an expert witness for the plaintiff. He brought along a completely detailed plastic model of the human eye. The jury literally leaned forward with interest as the ophthalmologist gave them an illustrated talk on the workings of the eye and how the accident had damaged the woman's vision. She won her case.

In personal injury cases, bodily demonstration is permitted at the discretion of the trial judge. The plaintiff may then exhibit his injuries to the jury and show how they've hindered or handicapped him.

Obviously, there are certain opportunities for histrionics here, and I suppose it's only human that some plaintiffs succumb to them. Attempts to bend a knee or manipulate a neck may elicit anything from a grimace of distress to a shriek of pain. However, when a plaintiff is allowed to exhibit an injury to the jury, the defendant is entitled to have an expert examine it.

While I'm against histrionics in court, there are times when a little showmanship will highlight a point for the jury. The medical witness who puts on an exhibit or demonstration, for example, is putting on a show. To gain maximum impact, it's permissible to emphasize your words and actions. Face the jury and address it directly. Gesture. Use a pointer if it's appropriate. If circumstances permit, move about a little. Above all, use words that laymen will understand.

A word of caution: Don't stand where you'll cut off the view of any of the jurors. A surprising number of witnesses do. The judge or the opposition attorney may stop your demonstration and request that you shift your position. That will have a halting effect on your testimony, especially if it happens repeatedly.

That kind of testifying calls for rehearsal. If you're planning to illustrate your testimony with an exhibit or demonstration, discuss the matter in advance with the lawyer concerned. Let him see the material involved, and let him help you decide the order in which it should be presented. Then run through the presentation until you feel comfortably familiar with it.

One final warning: If anything mechanical is involved in your exhibit, test the working parts just before you go into court. I well remember an internist who'd prepared an exhibit that depended largely on a slide projector. At the crucial moment in court, the machine became cantankerous, projecting slides upside down, sideways, and at other cockeyed angles. Finally, after much fiddling and muttering on the internist's part, the projector refused to work at all.

BACK UP YOUR WORDS WITH ILLUSTRATIONS

On another occasion, a medical witness who intended to use a large blackboard in court ran into a rather disconcerting difficulty. Every time he tried to press the chalk to the blackboard, the legs of the stand would collapse. By coincidence, the trial involved a man who'd been injured while drunk. After the blackboard had toppled for the third time—with the jury in stitches with suppressed laughter—the judge dryly remarked to the medical witness, "I think you'd better forget it, Doctor. The blackboard also seems to be under the influence."

In all fairness, I must admit that lawyers make their share of boo-boos in staging exhibits or demonstrations. In one case, a milkman was claiming damages for injuries sustained while mounting a short stairway leading into an apartment house lobby. The defense lawyer, trying to prove contributory negligence, had a reproduction of the stairway brought into court. His intention was to show how easy it was to skip up and down the steps. The intention was good, but his performance was bad. He slipped and broke a leg.

Slipups in court, unfortunately, are a sad fact of legal life. In the next chapter, I'll tell you how to avoid slipups with the judge and jury.

HOW TO ACT TOWARD JUDGE AND JURY

XIII

An irreverent Illinois Appellate judge once declared that "one of the greatest difficulties of the trial judge is to keep his mouth shut." Therefore, a medical witness shouldn't be surprised—as some are—if the judge pops a question at him. The judge, of course, has a right to intervene if he thinks the medical testimony needs to be clarified or expanded. Some judges do it often, others hardly at all. In any event, the medical witness should respond to any questions promptly, fully, and—above all—respectfully.

The need for respect may seem obvious. Yet many times I've seen medical witnesses react to a question from the judge as though their competence or integrity were being challenged. I've seen these doctors turn and frown or glare at the judge before replying to his question—and sometimes reply in a curt or contemptuous manner. In one extreme case, a crusty surgeon actually got into a hassle with the judge, and ended up by shouting, "You may know a lot about the law, but you don't know a damned thing about medicine!"

The surgeon then learned a bit more about the law. He was fined for contempt of court and dismissed as a witness.

No matter how great a figure of authority you are in your office or hospital, forget it when you take the witness stand. In court, there's only one boss, and that's the judge. He can say and do just about anything he pleases in his own court. If he says or does the wrong thing, he can be corrected on appeal—but that's no immediate help to you. Your sole concern is to give the best medical testimony you can, and you're not going to do that if you let the judge rile you.

I'm not saying that judges never do anything that gives the medical witness cause for irritation or anger. Some do—and occasionally in a flagrantly aggravating manner. If you should ever run up against one of those curmudgeons, do as wise old soldiers do when confronted by obnoxious officers: Salute the uniform, not the man. In other words, even if you hate the judge's guts, treat him or her with the deference due to a court of law.

Judges, of course, vary in personality just as much as other humans do. Some are warm and easy-going, others cold and aggressive. Most fall somewhere in between. I've found it useful to alert my medical witnesses in advance as to what sort of judge they'll be testifying before. Most lawyers are quite knowledgeable about the judges in their areas, and they'll be glad to pass along this knowledge if you request it.

On the stand, there are three circumstances under which you may address the judge:

1. If he asks you a question.

2. If the lawyer examining you seeks an answer that might be privileged. You're entitled to ask the judge whether you should or shouldn't answer.

3. If the cross-examiner demands a "Yes" or "No" answer, and you don't feel that it would be adequate, you may turn to the judge and tell him so. Most judges will allow you to give a fuller answer. Some won't—and in that case, *don't* argue about it. The lawyer for your

side can have you bring out the whole story on redirect examination.

If the judge breaks into cross-examination and queries the lawyer on why he's asking you a certain line of questions, listen carefully. The lawyer's reply will alert you to his intentions.

In my experience, practically all judges *try* to be impartial. Some, however, may inadvertently influence the jury through their demeanor, attitude, or voice inflection. That's why, when you're on the witness stand, it's so important to get along with the judge. The jury is inclined to side with the man or woman on the bench—and if he or she frowns at you, the jury may be frowning at you, too. In effect, the judge is the 13th juror.

As for jurors, they too come in all shapes and sizes, intellectually as well as physically.

Some, to put it kindly, are less than knowledgeable. I remember one case in which a medical witness was testifying at length about a bowel operation. He referred repeatedly to the "colon." After he'd left the stand, a frowning juror raised his hand and asked the judge, "What's a colon got to do with all this?" Subsequent questioning by the perplexed judge brought out the fact that the juror was aware of only one kind of colon—the punctuation mark.

Other jurors, unfortunately, are biased about certain matters; some may be outright bigots. Consider a West Coast malpractice case in which an obstetrician was accused of negligence and abandonment. The evidence was heavily in his favor. He had been busy with a delivery when another of his patients gave birth prematurely. The premature birth, which was difficult, had been handled by a G.P. with whom the obstetrician had an arrangement for such emergencies.

The obstetrician himself explained all this on the witness stand, and he seemed to make a good impression.

Nevertheless, the jury couldn't reach a decision. One member, it later turned out, had developed a strong distrust of the obstetrician because he wore a certain lodge pin in the lapel of his jacket. That single member made it a hung jury, stubbornly refusing to go along with the 11 others in a verdict favoring the obstetrician.

So if you're due to go on the witness stand, I'd advise you to remove any insignia that might antagonize a juror. Whatever your opinions about nonmedical matters, you'd be wise to keep them out of the courtroom. I interviewed a medical witness not long ago who was wearing a button bearing the slogan, "Support Your Local Police." He was surprised when I suggested that he remove it before taking the stand. "Who could be offended by a civic slogan like this?" he demanded.

The answer is, we just don't know who could be offended by what—and when a court case is involved, it's best not to take chances. The law, like medicine, works best in an atmosphere of trust. If a medical witness doesn't seem trustworthy to jurors—no matter how trivial the reason—he's in trouble.

He's in trouble, too, if he tries to impress the jury with his knowledge. A medical witness is judged not by how much he knows, but by how much the jury knows when he's finished testifying. One good way to put your testimony across, as I've emphasized throughout this book, is to avoid medical jargon and speak plain English. An even better way is to create graphic word pictures that get through to the simplest minds. The nervous system, for example, can be compared to a telephone switchboard; the heart to a pump; a sclerosed blood vessel to a rotten hose.

While jurors like to be addressed in language they can understand, they resent even the appearance of condescension. One medical witness I know, a professionally competent man but somewhat rough in his speech, made a bad impression on a jury because he used a lot of slang. "He talked to us as though we were a bunch of street-corner bums," a juror later complained.

Juries are also put off by medical witnesses who seem unconcerned or even callous about the suffering of a patient. I once heard an internist on the stand say of a plaintiff, "Sure, he's got a little pain, but it's not nearly as bad as he claims." The internist may well have been right, but the way he put it was wrong. It would have been more discreet to say, "In my experience with cases of this sort, I've found the level of pain to be low." The offhand phrase, "it's not nearly as bad as he claims," may have reminded jurors of unsympathetic doctors they'd known. In any event, they voted in favor of the plaintiff—and so, in effect, against that medical witness.

While a sympathetic manner is helpful to the medical witness in achieving rapport with the jury, it's also necessary to keep an eye on what *their* manner is. If you notice jurors looking bored, or even dozing, something's wrong with your delivery. Liven it up. Here's an example of what I mean:

In a Midwest case, a truckdriver claimed he'd suffered genital trouble after a highway crash. His expert medical witness, a rather pedantic urologist, identified the difficulty as Peyronie's disease. This medical term meant little or nothing to the jury. Worse, the witness went on with a long, rambling, monotonous general description of the disease, using such expressions as "a thickening of the fascial coverings in the erectile, vascular portions of the penis." Some jurors began to look dazed or drowsy—a danger signal that the witness either didn't notice or didn't care to notice.

The jury came wide awake, however, when the expert medical witness for the defense took the stand. He spoke crisply and specifically. Peyronie's disease, he explained, causes "a crooking of the penis during erection." The all-male jury was now all ears. Here was something they were interested in and wanted to know more about. They listened intently as the witness went on to describe how the angular penis would make normal sex relations difficult or impossible. The cause of the condition was not known, the doctor stated, but injury was rarely associated with it. In the case under consideration, he opined, the injury had probably only called attention to a preexisting condition.

The jurors were not only interested in what that medical witness was saying—they believed him. The verdict was in favor of the defense.

One important point on this matter of jury-watching: Don't make it obvious—don't stare at them. If you're giving answers that are short, address them to the lawyer asking the questions. If a query involves a lengthy, instructive answer—or if you're explaining an exhibit or demonstration—*then* address yourself to the jury. They're the ones who have to be instructed. Speak to them as you would to a group of your patients who need medical information.

At the same time, size them up. Single out the intelligent-looking members, or those who appear understanding. Concentrate on them—but not, of course, to the exclusion of the others. Move your gaze from face to face, only occasionally locking eyes with jurors who seem particularly receptive. If you can convince *them*, they'll usually argue for your side in the jury room.

I say "usually" because no one, no matter how expert, can always foretell what a particular juror is going to do. Melvin Belli, the noted California lawyer, tells a story about one of the first cases he ever tried. In his summing-up, he pulled out all the stops, throwing his heart and soul into the argument. The impassioned appeal obviously affected one of the jurors—a plump, middle-aged, motherly woman. She sat there with tears streaming down her cheeks. Well, Belli thought, at least I've got *her* on my side.

Later, when the jury verdict turned out to be unfavorable to him, Belli was flabbergasted to learn that the motherly juror *hadn't* sided with him. He sought her out and said, "But I thought you were in sympathy with me. Why were you crying?"

"Because," the woman explained, "you're so young and you were trying so hard, and I knew that I'd have to vote against you."

Well, nothing can be done about unpredictable jurors. Something *can* be done, however, to help you dodge pitfalls presented by privileged communications. We'll go into that subject in the next chapter.

XIV

WHAT YOU CAN AND CAN'T REVEAL ABOUT A PATIENT

The confidential nature of the doctor-patient relationship is well established. The Oath of Hippocrates states: "Whatever, in connection with my professional practice, or not in connection with it, I see, or hear, in the lives of men, which ought not to be spoken abroad, I will not divulge, as reckoning that all such should be kept secret." And Section 9 of the American Medical Association's Principles of Medical Ethics declares: "A physician may not reveal the confidence entrusted in him in the course of medical attendance, or the deficiencies he may observe in the character of patients, unless he is required to do so by law or unless it becomes necessary in order to protect the welfare of the individual or of the community."

The need for this confidential relationship is obvious: If a patient didn't feel free to tell all, the doctor would be hampered in diagnosing and treating the ailment. The doctor on the witness stand, however, should be aware of the distinct legal line drawn between "confidential" and "privileged" communication. "Confidential" pertains to the doctor's ethical duty to keep secret most information he might have obtained while attending a patient in a professional capacity. This information becomes "privileged" only if state law provides that it cannot be divulged in legal proceedings without the patient's consent.

While most states have such laws, they vary greatly in scope and content. If a medical witness has any doubts about whether he should or shouldn't reveal certain information about a patient, he'd be wise to check with the lawyer concerned before taking the stand. Then, if the doctor is asked a question that he knows he shouldn't respond to, he can say: "I ask to be excused from answering because the answer would violate my patient's confidence and invade the doctor-patient privilege."

Similarly, if a medical witness is unexpectedly asked a question that he thinks might be privileged, he can turn to the judge and say: "Your Honor, I doubt that I should answer that question. I believe it involves a confidential communication between doctor and patient."

The judge will then make a decision. Usually it's best to accept his ruling. However, if the medical witness feels strongly enough about the point under contention, he can insist on preserving the confidentiality of the patient communication. The results vary; some medical witnesses have been upheld on the grounds of privilege, but others haven't. In a recent case, a psychiatrist was jailed because he refused to comply with a judge's insistence that he divulge information about a patient that the physician felt was confidential.

Keep in mind that the "privilege" is for the protection of the patient and is not the right of the doctor. If the patient waives the privilege, the medical witness must testify as to relevant matters. The waiver can be explicit or tacit—that is (a) by the patient's written consent, (b) through a clause in an insurance policy, or (c) by implication in a personal injury suit, where the patient himself reveals the details of his injuries. A patient also relinquishes the privilege if he's on trial for a crime, or if he sues a physician for medical malpractice.

WHAT YOU CAN AND CAN'T REVEAL ABOUT A PATIENT

The patient's privilege extends to medical records and written communications that include references to confidential matters. Thus, whenever you're requested by a patient to testify in a legal action and to make your records available to other parties, it's advisable to get the patient's signature on a consent form similar to the following:

> *I, the undersigned, authorize Dr. ______________ to reveal information relative to his diagnosis and treatment of me between the dates of ______________ and ______________. This authorization extends to records and written communications.*
>
> *Also, in any legal action to which I am or may become a party, I authorize Dr. ______________ to testify as to his medical findings and treatment of me. Further, in behalf of myself or any persons who may have interest in the matter, I hereby waive all provisions of the law relative to the disclosure of confidential medical information.*

This should be signed by the patient and a witness, with a note of the date and place of signature.

Sometimes a patient may give an insurance adjuster or lawyer a memorandum waiving privilege and authorizing you to discuss the case. If such a memo is presented, you cannot refuse to disclose what the patient told you or to withhold his medical records. In your own interest, however, you should take the following four precautions:

1. Be sure the paper is signed by your patient.

2. Make certain that it actually waives privilege and authorizes you to release pertinent information without limitation.

3. For filing purposes, keep the paper, or get a photostatic copy. Attach a memorandum of your own, relating what you told the third party.

4. Finally, if you have any doubt at all about the waiver, check it by phone with your patient.

More than a few doctors on the witness stand have discovered that privilege doesn't cover as wide an area as they had thought. For example, in a divorce case, a physician declined to reveal symptoms that a golfing companion had told him about. The court held that privilege didn't apply because there was no physician-patient relationship or employment; the exchange had simply been a "social discussion" on the golf course. Thus, the doctor was compelled to divulge the symptoms, which indicated that the golfing companion had been suffering from a venereal disease.

Here are other circumstances in which the physician-patient privilege does not apply:

When you're called to attend a patient and he tells you something that's not relevant to diagnosis or treatment. Let's say a workman has been injured in a fall from a structural scaffold. While you're examining him, he blurts: "It's all my fault! There was nothing wrong with that scaffold! I jumped off it because my wife has left me! I felt so low I just decided to end it all!" If you were called to testify in a subsequent divorce action, or perhaps a suit the worker might file against the construction contractor, you would not be able to claim privilege if asked about the nonmedical things the workman had told you.

When an insurance company employs you to examine a claimant. This usually is solely for the purpose of examination, with no treatment involved. Consequently there is no doctor-patient relationship, and the information obtained is not privileged.

When you examine a person to assess his physical fitness for certain work, or to determine his eligibility for a pension, or to adjudicate an application for insurance. Again, since no treatment takes place, there is no privilege.

When the information is not of a confidential nature. The mere fact that a physician has treated a given patient, for example, cannot be withheld on the grounds of privilege;

the doctor can even give the number of visits and the dates.

Furthermore, it has generally been held that privilege is not violated if a doctor reveals the names of patients. There's a fine legal distinction here, though; violation *would* occur if the revelation contained anything relative to diagnosis or treatment. This distinction was neatly clarified in the following California case:

A physician and a hospital were sued for damages by a patient who claimed he had been injured as the result of an angiogram examination. In an attempt to strengthen his case, the patient sought the names and addresses of 16 patients of the physician who had received the same test; he wanted to interview those patients and get them to discuss their experiences. The trial court granted the patient's motion.

That decision was reversed by the Court of Appeals of California. The higher court ruled that, while the disclosure of patients' names ordinarily wouldn't violate the doctor-patient privilege, it would in this case. The reason: Revealing the names would also disclose the confidential information that the patients had received a specified examination.

Admittedly, the rules of privilege occasionally can be tough to understand. Some cross-examiners can be tough, too—a problem that we'll tackle next.

HOW TO HANDLE A TOUGH CROSS-EXAMINER

XV

Keep cool on the hot seat. That's the most effective way for the medical witness to deal with the cross-examiner who comes on too strong. Here's an illustration of what I mean:

Dr. James A. Brussel, the noted psychiatrist and crime consultant, was once testifying in a case in which the mental condition of a patient was at issue. Brussel had interviewed the man at length before the trial, and from the witness chair he told of his findings. The cross-examiner, a very aggressive lawyer, demanded, "Is that all he told you?"

"No, not quite."

"Well, let's have it all. What else did he tell you?"

"I'd rather not say. It's nothing important."

The cross-examiner closed in for the kill. "Doctor, that's not for you to decide! I insist on an answer!"

"Go chase yourself!" Brussel retorted.

After a stunned silence, uproar broke out in the court. Much of it came from the outraged cross-examiner, who loudly called on the judge to do something about the "impertinent" medical witness. When the psychiatrist had explained the situation, however, it was the aggressive cross-examiner who looked foolish. Brussel had simply repeated the patient's parting remark to him, and there was no doubt that the cross-examiner had asked for it.

Not many medical witnesses get such a good opportunity to defuse a bombastic attorney in court. There are, however, many ways to take at least some of the steam out of an over-forceful cross-examiner.

One is to challenge any question that contains a misrepresentation or falsehood. For example, in another of the many cases in which Dr. Brussel has appeared as a medical witness, a former mental patient was suspected of having assaulted a woman on the fourth floor of a suburban apartment house. The accused man was also crippled. His lawyer brought out during the course of the trial that the apartment house had no elevator. Brussel then testified that in his opinion the crippled man was capable of climbing the stairs.

The cross-examiner exploded. Slamming a fist into the palm of his hand, he shouted, "Doctor, do you mean to say that this crippled man could have walked from his rooming house in the heart of the city all the way out to the suburb, climbed those four flights of stairs, committed the alleged crime, then gone back down the stairs and walked back to his rooming house?"

A less experienced witness might have become flustered by this heated attack, but Brussel kept his cool. "No," he replied, "I don't mean to say any such thing. I gave my opinion that the defendant is capable of climbing the four flights of stairs. I don't know how he got to the apartment house. He may not necessarily have walked there."

Subsequent testimony from other witnesses bore that out; the defendant had been given a lift in a car to and from the suburb.

Actually, the browbeating type of lawyer is disappearing. There are still some around, though, and the medical witness should know how to deal with one. The way to meet an attack of this kind is to apply the principles of judo, in which an assailant is defeated largely through the force of his own assault. Never let yourself be provoked to counterattack. Always retain your dignity, and it will show up the cross-examiner for what he really is—a bully. Be polite, but also be resilient. If an opportunity occurs to turn the cross-examiner's antics against him, take advantage of it.

For example, an internist who was testifying for a plaintiff represented by a friend of mine came under an almost savage attack from the cross-examiner. The lawyer rushed at the medical witness, shook a finger in his face, and started shouting questions. My friend was about to object when the internist neatly took care of the situation himself. In a mild tone of voice, he said to the lawyer, "Counsel, would you mind standing back and lowering your voice? You're so close and making so much noise that I can't address my remarks to the jury." Thus, in his own quiet way, the internist did more than put the lawyer in his place. He also allied himself with the jury and gained their favor.

In another case, Dr. Maurice H. Herzmark, a Washington, D.C., orthopedic surgeon, was testifying for a man who'd been struck in the back by a taxi. The cross-examiner demanded at one point that Herzmark demonstrate on himself where the sacroiliac joint is located.

"It's too deep," the medical witness replied. "It won't show."

"Well, I'll show you where the sacroiliac is!" the lawyer declared. He lifted the rear part of his jacket, backed up to the witness stand, and began slapping the area where he believed the sacroiliac joint to be located. "Isn't that where it is, Doctor? Isn't that where it is?"

"Well," said Herzmark, putting on his glasses and peering at the cross-examiner, "from where I sit, it seems to me you're patting yourself on the buttock."

The laugh, of course, was on the young lawyer. Because of his own belligerent behavior, he'd been made to look foolish.

Let me stress right here that I'm not advising medical witnesses to strive for humor in court. Far from it. I've seen attempts at jokes and wisecracks on the witness stand backfire too often. All I'm saying is that if a wild-swinging cross-examiner leaves himself open to one of his own blows, let him have it. This can be done only by the medical witness who keeps calm and alert.

On the other hand, of course, the medical witness who leaves *himself* open to a backlash is also asking for trouble. During the course of a California case that involved an eye injury, an ophthalmologist kept referring to collyrium in his testimony. On cross-examination, the lawyer said, "Doctor, I happen to know what collyrium is, but perhaps the jury doesn't. Would you explain what it is?"

"Why, it's eyewash."

The lawyer raised one eyebrow and said, "You mentioned it at least a dozen times in your testimony. That's a lot of eyewash."

A snide remark? Sure, but it brought guffaws from the jury and made the medical witness look silly. He could have avoided the whole embarrassing episode by (1) testifying in plain English; (2) keeping in mind that the lawyer might have studied up on the medical terms involved; and (3) regarding the cross-examiner as an experienced faultfinder.

If you're due to appear in court as a medical witness, ask the attorney on your side what the opposition lawyer is like. That will give you some idea of what to expect. Attorneys who appear in medico-legal cases are pretty well known to each other.

Even if they're not, they can often find out. For example, prior to one case in which I was defending a doctor, I met the plaintiff's lawyer for the first time. I asked him casually how many witnesses he expected to call.

"Oh, a whole bunch," he said. "Possibly dozens."

"Including the paint salesman from Terre Haute?"

"Oh, sure. I got a terrific statement out of him."

Well, there was no paint salesman from Terre Haute. I had put the question as a joke—in responding seriously, the lawyer had revealed himself as a bluffer. That information was helpful to my client when he came under cross-examination.

Some tough cross-examiners try to pressure medical witnesses into committing a common fault—becoming too emphatic in their statements, or overly defensive of their testimony. One G.P., badgered by the cross-examiner about a certain medical point, finally shouted, "I'd swear to it!"

"Doctor," the lawyer snapped, "what did you think you were doing during the rest of your testimony?"

The doctor tried to sputter an explanation, but the cross-examiner dismissed him. The lawyer had succeeded in his aim—to make the jury doubt the medical witness's reliability. If the G.P. had stuck to his contention calmly, he'd have made a far better impression.

Probably the toughest type of cross-examiner is the one who doesn't appear tough at all. He may be all smiles and good humor. He might even crack a joke or two. Then, with the atmosphere relaxed, he lets fly with a surprise question. That often clobbers the medical witness who's been lulled into a sense of security. The solution: When a cross-examiner comes on in a friendly fashion, don't lower your guard—raise it.

Beware, too, of the cross-examiner who tries to slip into your good graces. He may also be trying to slip a false insinuation into your testimony. Here's an example:

On the East Coast, an orthopedist was testifying in a personal injury case. On direct examination, he gave his expert medical opinion that the plaintiff would be afflicted by a limp for the rest of his life. The cross-examiner, a plump little lawyer with a very pleasant manner, commented in flattering terms on the orthopedist's background and qualifications. He also congratulated him on his "brilliant" testimony.

Then he smiled and said, "But isn't it true, Doctor, that medicine is an inexact science?"

The orthopedist, obviously won over by the cross-examiner, replied, "Yes, that's true."

"And isn't it also true that a medical opinion involves a certain amount of speculation?"

The witness hesitated, then gave in to the winning smile of the nice little lawyer, "Yes."

"And speculation, of course, is merely guesswork," the cross-examiner concluded briskly. "That's all, Doctor."

Thus, a pall of doubt was cast over the orthopedist's testimony. His mistake was in allowing himself to be taken in by the word "speculation."

If you're ever on the witness stand and the cross-examiner tries to get you to agree that your opinion is speculation or guesswork, *disagree.* Say, "No, my opinion is based on reasonable medical certainty and in accordance with scientific probability."

There's another type of cross-examiner to beware of—the sort who specializes in silent threats. He may approach the witness stand while grimly shuffling a batch of papers. When you come up against that sort, ignore his paper-shuffling. He's only trying to frighten you into thinking those papers contain damaging evidence. Ignore, too, the opposition lawyer who showily writes down some of your responses. He's probably only striving to give the impression that he's going to make you eat your words.

In contrast to such silent gimmicks, there's the cross-examiner who goes in for noisy histrionics. "Crying Dan," a weepy lawyer who practiced in San Francisco many years ago, is a good example of the type. His lugubrious cross-examinations and arguments became so well known that a judge once told him, "Dan, I'm going to allow you one hour for argument. That will give you 15 minutes for your summation and 45 for crying."

There aren't many "Crying Dans" around these days, but there are still quite a few courtroom thespians who simulate disbelief, amazement, indignation, and outrage while cross-examining a medical witness. Don't let their antics upset you. That's exactly what they're designed to do. Just be careful to pause briefly before replying to their questions. Quite often this flamboyant type of cross-examiner goes beyond the bounds of proper legal procedure, and that pause will permit the lawyer for your side to object.

Finally, *never* lose your temper under cross-examination. An angry witness is a careless witness—or, as the Bible puts it: "He that is soon angered dealeth foolishly." One doctor learned that the hard way when he tangled with the noted trial lawyer Melvin Belli. The doctor was fuming as he left the stand after a scorching cross-examination. "Mr. Belli," he growled, "let me congratulate you on a very superficial knowledge of medicine."

Belli bowed and responded, "Doctor, I would like to go at least as far as you. But honesty does not permit it." In sum, it's dangerous to cross verbal swords with a lawyer; he's probably armed with many more cutting words than you are.

WATCH OUT FOR THESE BOOBY TRAPS

XVI

Some medical witnesses start out on the stand as Dr. Jekyll and wind up as Mr. Hyde. During direct examination, they are relaxed, pleasant, and cooperative. As soon as the cross-examiner approaches them, however, they visibly tense up—scowling and leaning forward belligerently. Under cross-examination, they respond overemphatically in a raised voice. Instead of a simple "Yes" or "No," they come out with a loud "Positively!" or "Absolutely not!" As a result, the jury is left with the unfortunate impression that the witness is struggling to make doubtful testimony sound convincing.

This is one of many pitfalls some medical witnesses stumble into that can weaken a strong case. To avoid that one, *don't* change your demeanor or tone of voice when you go from direct to cross-examination. That's equally important if you happen to have a bit of Caspar Milquetoast in you, rather than Mr. Hyde. Some doctors shrink from the heat of a scorching cross-examination. They may even cringe or look flustered. The question then arises in the minds of the jury: *Why* is this fellow so worried and nervous?

Another potential booby trap is the fondness some lawyers have for arranging a system of signals with their medical witnesses. For example: if the cross-examiner touches on a particular medical issue but doesn't bring it out enough, the witness is supposed to stroke his chin, or tug an ear. That means the lawyer for the doctor's side should develop the issue on redirect examination. Personally, I'm against the signal system. A good attorney can quickly spot and expose it, thus making the doctor on the stand seem to be a conspirator.

It's unwise, too, for a physician to disparage the medical expert for the opposing side during cross-examination. If the expert is open to criticism or attack, that's a job for a lawyer to handle, not a doctor. When a doctor does it, he sounds petty or vindictive to the jury. It's advisable to say something like, "I'm sure Dr. Jones is a competent physician, but I simply don't agree with him on this particular issue."

If the cross-examiner himself seems inept or ill-informed on the medical matters involved, the witness may be tempted to be scornful or patronizing. Don't give in to this temptation. There *are* inept and ill-informed attorneys, but it's best for the medical witness to regard all cross-examiners as good ones. Even a third-rate boxer occasionally gets in a lucky punch and knocks out a champion.

There are three situations in which the medical witness must be especially careful to keep his guard up during cross-examination:

1. When the cross-examiner turns away as though he's finished with the witness. That tends to relax the doctor, just as a prizefighter relaxes when he hears the bell. The cross-examiner may then quickly turn back, with the "Just a moment—one more question" tactic. The question will probably be a tough one, and the medical witness who's caught with his defenses down may be hit hard. Don't relax or lower your guard until the cross-examiner says, "That is all, Doctor."

2. When the cross-examiner starts a series of short, rapid-fire questions calling for, say, repeated "Yes" answers. The careless medical witness often falls into the rhythm and is caught unaware if the lawyer unexpectedly asks a question calling for a "No" answer. Even if the doctor recovers and gives the correct answer, the jury is left with an impression of carelessness.

WATCH OUT FOR THESE BOOBY TRAPS

3. When the cross-examiner starts off a question with, "It's a fact." It may not be a fact, and if it's not, say so at once.

Some cross-examiners are adept at slipping in a double question. The first question may call for a "No" answer, the second for a "Yes." The natural inclination of the medical witness is to answer the second question first, thus giving the cross-examiner a chance to move quickly on, leaving the impression that Yes is the answer to both questions. Sometimes this tactic works, sometimes it doesn't. Here's one instance in which it didn't work:

The doctor on the stand was a rural G.P. who could have been typecast for the role in a movie. His hair was white and shaggy. He kept peering over his eyeglasses. And he had a kindly smile.

The cross-examiner, a brisk young lawyer, asked a series of innocuous questions. The G.P. answered them routinely.

Then the cross-examiner slipped in a double question: "The plaintiff is making a good recovery under your care, isn't he—he *is* still under your care, isn't he?"

The G.P. was too cagy to take that bait. He smiled kindly at the cross-examiner and said, "Well, sir, let's take first things first. The patient is *not* making a good recovery. However, he *is* still under my care."

Occasionally, when a cross-examiner is unable to shake the testimony of a medical witness, he may try to cast doubt on the doctor's credibility. In an East Coast personal injury case, an internist was testifying about treatment he had given the plaintiff some five years previously. On cross-examination, he stuck by his testimony.

The cross-examiner then remarked: "Doctor, all that happened five years ago, and yet you can recall everything in detail. You seem to have a remarkable memory."

"It's fair."

"All right, let's test it. How many times have you been married, Doctor?"

The lawyer for the doctor's side immediately objected, claiming the question was irrelevant. When the cross-examiner insisted that he was simply trying to check the witness's memory, the judge allowed the question to stand.

The internist then responded, "Three times."

"State the maiden name of your second wife."

The unexpected question left the internist gaping. For the life of him, he couldn't remember the maiden name of a woman to whom he'd been married only briefly about a dozen years ago. To gain time, he started to stammer something, but the cross-examiner cut him off. "That will be all, Doctor! That will be all!"

You may not have managed to include three wives in your career, but here are some other instances in which a cross-examiner may try to cast doubt on your testimony:

If you've been the longtime physician of the person you're testifying for. The usual approach is for the cross-examiner to suggest you're a friend of the patient. The correct answer: "I hope I'm a friend to all my patients." If the cross-examiner persists and asks whether you'd like to see your "friend" win the case, reply "I'm here to give impartial medical testimony, not to decide who is legally right or wrong. I'm sure the jury is capable of doing that."

If you're testifying out of your field. In that situation, better be sure you can prove you know what you're talking about.

If you appear frequently as a medical witness. Some cross-examiners are quick to question the credibility of doctors who testify often as expert medical witnesses. One favorite query is: "Doctor, you're something of a professional witness, aren't you?" The correct answer: "No, my profession is the practice of medicine (or surgery). It just so happens that I'm frequently called to testify on medical matters." One other point: Doctors who testify often should make themselves available to both plaintiffs and defendants. If possible, they should also avoid working over and over for the same legal counsel. A medical witness of this type soon gets the reputation of being "Attorney So-and-So's house doctor."

WATCH OUT FOR THESE BOOBY TRAPS

If you've come a long distance to testify as an expert medical witness. Again, be prepared to explain why a local doctor wasn't obtained. The explanation is usually quite simple. There may not be a local doctor who qualifies as an expert medical witness in this particular case. Or your qualifications may be especially suited to the issues involved.

Some medical witnesses are inclined to get quite exasperated under prolonged cross-examination, especially when the questions of the lawyer seem tortuous and time-wasting. Just remember that when a lawyer stretches out cross-examination, it usually means that he hasn't been able to break down your testimony and he's getting desperate. To help you keep your composure, you might also remember John Quincy Adams's definition of "law logic" as "an artificial system of reasoning, exclusively used in courts of justice, but good for nothing anywhere else."

Keep in mind, too, that words are a lawyer's stock in trade. Shades of meaning are important in his world of "law logic," and he's going to try to turn up the shade that makes his side look best. For example, if you refer on the witness stand to a patient's "symptom," the cross-examiner may say, "That's what the plaintiff *told* you, isn't it?" You should reply, "It's what I found out through medical examination, which includes questioning of the patient." And don't get agitated by this word battle, which may strike you as nitpicking.

Finally, while you're on the witness stand, never lose sight of the fact that *you're* the expert. In trying to set a trap for you, the cross-examiner may fall into the trap himself. I saw a splendid example of this during a recent trip to England. It happened in a London court, where the cross-examiner was trying to break down the testimony of a music expert in a case involving the alleged infringement of a song copyright.

The cross-examiner, a very aggressive barrister, had been knighted because of his professional achievements. At one point, he hotly insisted, "Now pray, sir, don't beat about the bush, but explain precisely what you mean by accent in music."

The expert coolly responded: "Accent in music is a certain stress laid upon a particular note. This can be compared to the way in which stress is laid upon a given word for the purpose of better understanding. Thus, if I were to say, 'You are an *ass*,' the accent rests on 'ass.' But if I were to say, '*You* are an ass,' the accent rests on 'you,' Sir John."

Even if you come through your testimony with flying colors, as that music expert did, it doesn't necessarily mean that there aren't any more traps left before you leave the courtroom. We'll get down to the final precautions in the next and concluding chapter.

DON'T SPOIL IT WITH A POOR FINISH

XVII

During a trial in the Midwest, an internist was called to testify for one of his patients, a housewife who'd been injured in a car crash. The woman was asking $100,000 damages, contending that her injuries kept her from doing heavy household chores. This contention was supported by the internist, who described the injuries in detail on direct examination. The cross-examiner was unable to shake the internist's testimony, and the witness was dismissed. He then made his first and only mistake—but it was a costly one. In passing the plaintiff and her attorney, he flashed them the V-for-victory sign. The jury saw it, and they obviously figured the doctor was biased. They awarded the woman only $5,000 damages.

Most medical witnesses are more discreet. Many, however, unthinkingly weaken or destroy their testimony by giving vent to their feelings as they leave the stand. Some mop their brow, or sigh deeply in relief. Others, sensing they've bested the opposition, grin broadly in triumph.

Among the worst offenders is the medical witness who scuttles away from the stand with unseemly haste. Sometimes the court isn't even finished with him. In a case not long ago, I saw a medical witness bolt for the exit as soon as the cross-examiner had concluded his questions. The lawyer for the doctor's side had to call him back to the stand for redirect examination.

The medical witness should stay seated after cross-examination. Quite often he'll be subjected to redirect examination, which gives him an opportunity to correct or explain matters drawn out by the cross-examiner. He should leave the stand only when he's told he may do so.

On rare occasions an attorney may request that the medical witness remain in court and sit at his table to advise him on technical matters. Otherwise, the witness should leave the court without pausing to talk with the attorney or other parties involved. Under no circumstances should he sit with the spectators after testifying. The jury might take this to mean that the doctor has a partisan interest in the outcome of the trial.

Unfortunately, if the doctor's day in court has been unpleasant or frustrating, he may be inclined to agree with a doctor-lawyer who once declared: "To the physician, the courtroom means wasting valuable time to give a carefully restricted opinion, necessarily based on inadequate observation, for persons who cannot understand the details of the problems and who probably will not believe them anyway."

That doctor-lawyer undoubtedly had his tongue firmly in cheek when he made that declaration. As I've attempted to show throughout this book, testifying in court doesn't necessarily have to be an ordeal. It can be a satisfying experience—*if* the medical witness places himself in the right frame of mind and follows the proper guidelines. Here's a handy rundown on the principal ones:

○ *Don't run scared.* Before you go to court, forget all those horror stories you may have heard about the terrors of testifying. As a medical witness, you'll be well protected. The jury will be more inclined to identify with you than with the cross-examiner. The judge will be watching out for your interests. And the lawyer for your side will be ready to jump to your assistance if the opposition attorney gets out of line. As for the opposition attorney himself, he'll be wary about tangling with an expert of your stature—unless you give him good reason for doing so.

DON'T SPOIL IT WITH A POOR FINISH

○ *Do your homework.* If you go to the witness stand without preparation, you're almost certain to run into trouble. Insist on a pretrial conference with the lawyer for your side. Find out what kind of medical witness you're to be—the "fact" type or the "opinion" type. Ask the lawyer what medical theory he hopes to prove, then go over the facts and ascertain whether they support the theory. If they do, map out with the lawyer the best strategy for presenting the case in court. To bolster your testimony, read all pertinent medical records, documents, and reports. It's also wise to check the literature on the medical problem involved.

○ *Don't try to dodge a deposition hearing.* It may seem like a nuisance to you, but giving a pretrial deposition can be a benefit. If both sides are impressed by your testimony, they may decide to settle out of court—or to accept your deposition for introduction at the trial, which means you won't have to attend. But keep this in mind while you're making your deposition: Although the hearing is informal, you're under oath and subject to all the responsibilities of testifying in court. Don't make any remarks that you wouldn't want repeated in court.

○ *Leave no doubt about your fee.* If you don't know the lawyer or claimant in the case, it's advisable to get a written agreement on your witness fee. The best way to compute the fee is on an hourly basis. This varies from area to area and depends largely on the expertise of the witness. In most cases, the hourly rate runs between $150 and $300. Include the time spent in making out reports, attending pretrial conferences, doing research, giving testimony at deposition hearings, and appearing in court. On the average, all that usually adds up to between 10 and 20 hours.

○ *Put your nervousness to work for you.* Many medical witnesses are keyed-up when they take the stand; that's only natural. Unfortunately, some succumb to stage fright. The best witnesses not only control their nervousness—they use it to make themselves sharp and alert. Here are three tips on how to do that:

(i) As you approach the stand, keep your eyes on the clerk who's waiting to administer the oath. This will help you to ward off feelings of distraction or distress caused by getting up before a roomful of spectators.

(ii) When you sit down, place the lower part of your back firmly against the back of the witness chair. Set both feet flat on the floor. Clasp your hands lightly and lean forward just a little. This position, many witnesses tell me, helps to hold nervousness in check.

(iii) Think of the jury as a group of your patients who need a medical problem explained. Address them as you would patients, thus placing yourself in a familiar role. As the doctor-patient feeling takes over, the tensions of the courtroom will gradually begin to fade away.

○ *Be careful of your dress and demeanor.* Jury decisions are sometimes influenced by such seemingly trivial matters as a cocky expression or a flashy necktie. Don't wear anything that's likely to divert jurors' attention from what you're saying. Make sure your clothing is comfortable. Look relaxed but serious. And don't mumble; speak clearly in a tone that will reach the farthest juror.

○ *Make the most of direct examination.* Although you're in the hands of a friendly lawyer, you can still make mistakes. Don't answer questions too quickly or too slowly. Don't volunteer more than you're asked for. Be specific. Use graphic, precise terms, but avoid medical jargon.

○ *Keep your records in good shape.* Remember that when you use your records to refresh your memory on the stand, they become part of the evidence. This means that the opposition lawyer can examine them, comment on them, or read from them. Consequently, don't put anything in your records that you wouldn't want read out in court. Remember that sloppy records will reflect unfavorably on you.

DON'T SPOIL IT WITH A POOR FINISH

For court purposes, good records should contain all pertinent dates, source of the patient visit, nature of the complaint, results of the examination, the diagnosis, the treatment prescribed, and the prognosis.

○ *Back up your testimony with exhibits and demonstrations.* If there are any visual means of adding weight to your words, use them. The most commonly used exhibit is the X-ray film. Others are graphs, charts, diagrams, and photographs.

Demonstrations with plastic torsos, artificial limbs, skeletons, and models of other parts of the anatomy are highly effective. You might also illustrate your testimony with drawings on a blackboard.

○ *Be alert to the mood of the judge and jury.* Practically all judges try to be impartial, but some may inadvertently influence the jury through their attitude toward a medical witness. That's one good reason you should try to get along with the judge. If he scowls at you, the jury may be scowling, too. Before you go to court, it would be a good idea to ask your lawyer what sort of judge you'll be up against.

When you address the jury, size them up. Concentrate on the intelligent-looking members, but not to the exclusion of others. Move your gaze from juror to juror, occasionally locking eyes with those who seem especially receptive. Convince *them* of what you are saying, and they will argue for your side in the jury room.

○ *Beware of cross-examination pitfalls.* Although the blustering type of attorney is disappearing, you just might run up against one. If you do, don't be provoked into an angry counterattack. Keep calm and dignified. That will show up the truculent cross-examiner for exactly what he is—a blowhard. Watch out, too, for the following types of cross-examiner:

1. The sort who's all smiles and friendliness. He may be trying to lull you into a false sense of security—just before clobbering you with a surprise question.

2. The kind who specializes in silent threats. He might approach the witness stand while grimly going through a pile of papers. Ignore the paper-shuffling. He's only trying to make you think he has a pile of damaging evidence.

3. The courtroom actor who simulates profound amazement, indignation, disbelief, and outrage while questioning you. Disregard his antics. They're principally designed to upset you.

No matter what sort of cross-examiner you encounter, don't change your demeanor or tone of voice when he takes over. Some medical witnesses visibly tense up. They scowl or frown, and their responses become overemphatic. As a result, the jury may get the impression that the witness is struggling to defend shaky testimony.

If you disagree with the medical expert for the opposing side, don't attack him. Simply state the points on which you disagree. If the opposition medical expert is open to attack, leave that to the lawyer for your side. It will sound vindictive if you do it.

Finally, don't get exasperated under prolonged cross-examination, particularly if the lawyer's questions seem tortuous and time-consuming. It merely means that he hasn't been able to weaken your testimony and he's getting desperate. Keep your head, keep your cool—and, when you're dismissed, leave the witness stand in a dignified manner.

If you keep those guidelines firmly in mind, you probably won't dread a court appearance. You may even welcome it. It *can* be a stimulating, rewarding experience.

APPENDIX

APPENDIX

A MALPRACTICE TRIAL THROUGH THE JURY'S EYES

The following account of post-trial interviews with the jurors in a $4.5 million malpractice suit provides a revealing look at some of the things—aside from the evidence—that influenced their verdict. Robert Cassidy, Midwest Editor of Medical Economics *conducted the interviews and wrote this account, which first appeared in the May 16, 1983, issue of the magazine.*

What makes a malpractice jury decide for or against a doctor? Apart from the evidence presented, what makes a lasting impression on jurors in the courtroom? And how do those impressions help shape their deliberations—and the verdict itself?

To get answers to those questions, I interviewed the jurors in a malpractice case against two physicians and a hospital. The suit was brought by the family of a woman who died several years after intestinal bypass surgery. The complaint alleged that the patient had suffered a number of postoperative complications, including kidney failure, and had to return to the hospital repeatedly.

The physicians named in the suit, a surgeon and an internist, were accused of failing to monitor the patient's condition, failing to reverse the operation after complications developed, and failing to call in kidney specialists and other consultants in time.

The trial lasted an exhausting 10 weeks and included testimony from more than 30 witnesses. My interviews with jurors indicate that the demeanor and credibility of the defendants, the reliability of expert witnesses, and the behavior of lawyers on both sides all had a significant impact on their perceptions of the case.

It was also clear that the jurors, who ranged in age from 25 to 65 and in occupation from motorcycle mechanic to welfare caseworker, evaluated the testimony by relating it to their everyday experiences. As employees they were expected to do their jobs. As jurors they had to determine whether or not the doctors were doing *their* jobs.

The internist did not make a favorable impression on most jurors. "Cocky," "arrogant," and "pompous" were among the words they used to describe him. "He seemed to be saying, 'I can do no wrong, I don't make mistakes.' Well, hey, he's human," said a 46-year-old bank operations officer.

"He had an I-don't-care attitude," added a 29-year-old secretary. "There was a glass of water by the witness stand, and when he drank from it, it was as if he were sitting in a bar, very casual. It was as if he had all the answers before he went on trial."

A 29-year-old printshop supervisor who became the jury foreman said, "I thought to myself, here's somebody who may be in serious trouble, and yet he's still arrogant. I was surprised by his attitude."

"He'd put his eyeglasses in his mouth, and when he got a tough question to answer, he'd chomp down on them," recalled a 25-year-old motorcycle mechanic. "Then when he went to read something, he'd make a big deal out of putting his glasses on, but he wouldn't even read what he was handed."

What bothered the jurors most was the doctor's seeming evasiveness. "He deliberately answered questions in a roundabout way, always tagging on an extra paragraph to vindicate himself," said a 25-year-old salesman. "If the plaintiff's attorney asks you a Yes or No question, you should answer Yes or No; later, your lawyer can let you expand. But he kept going on and on. He was only hurting himself."

The jurors had considerably more sympathy for the surgeon-defendant. "I liked him," one juror said. "He seemed to be of the old school." Another, a 28-year-old warehouse worker, said: "He reminded me of some doctors I had when I was a kid, quiet in manner and extremely concerned about his patients. He was a nice guy in a tight situation." Most of the jurors concurred in that assessment.

The internist's admission that he had changed hospital records damaged his credibility with several jurors. The plaintiff's attorney produced blowups of a prescription to show how the internist had crossed out a zero and moved a comma to reduce the dosage shown. He had also changed his own chart notes to make it appear that he had prescribed a smaller dosage.

A 43-year-old autoworker said, "He was trying to cover up." A steelworker, 42, added, "You must feel pretty guilty if you do something like that." And the jury foreman: "It certainly didn't help his case any."

Nor were the jurors impressed by the internist's primary defense: that the woman's kidneys had been damaged by streptomycin ordered by another physician to relieve a lung condition.

The jurors cited testimony by the defense's own expert witness that there was nothing in the medical literature of the previous 10 years to back the streptomycin argument, and that the effects of the drug would be felt for no more than several hours. "If he believed streptomycin was the cause, why didn't he write it down on her chart?" asked the jury foreman. "And when her condition got worse, even after she was off streptomycin, why didn't he do something about it?"

The secretary on the jury panel said simply, "I think he made up the streptomycin argument because that was the only leg he could stand on."

Jurors also took the internist to task for not calling in other specialists much sooner. The kidney specialist was not consulted until three years after the woman's surgery (but five years before her death). A 62-year-old welfare caseworker said, "If the internist didn't know why she was getting worse, why didn't he get someone else to help?"

The motorcycle mechanic related the case to his workaday world. "If I'm working on a bike with an ignition problem, I'll check the spark plug first, but if that doesn't work, I try something else. The doctor never bothered to check out other possibilities for the cause of the kidney failure."

The surgeon had some credibility problems, too. He failed to produce records of his conversations with the patient, claiming they'd been lost when he'd moved to another state. "That sounded fishy to me," said the secretary. "I work in an office, and I don't believe that records get lost. They can be misplaced, but they simply don't get lost."

At another point in the trial, the surgeon denied knowing anything about creatinine clearance tests. The plaintiff's attorney then pulled out of his briefcase a book that the surgeon had edited and pointed to a chapter on that subject. "The attorney caught him dead to rights," said the salesman.

The newness of the operation—the patient was the surgeon's second intestinal bypass patient—also weighed against him. "That bothered me very much," said the welfare caseworker. "He should have been watching her that much more closely."

A 55-year-old machinist said, "When I build a new piece of equipment, I watch it carefully, especially in the beginning. That's what these doctors were doing. They were dealing with a new type of surgery, and they should have been extra careful."

The surgeon actually saw the patient more frequently postoperatively than the internist did and the jurors found fault with him, as they did with the internist, for not turning to a consultant earlier. "Why was he taking care of her if he wasn't doing anything for her?" asked the steelworker.

The jurors were impressed by the medical experts on both sides. "One of the smartest men I've ever heard," said the jury foreman, referring to a professor of medicine who had testified for the plaintiffs. "He knew what he was talking about, but he could talk at our level and still use technical language."

Despite the awe in which they held the experts, the jurors refused to be dazzled by their testimony. Several, for example, said the professor lost some credibility because he admitted on the stand that he'd twice failed his boards. "He was a good witness, but his credentials weren't the greatest," said the steelworker.

The jurors also had mixed feelings about a defense expert, a top-notch researcher who testified that the internist could not be held liable for the patient's kidney failure. Why? Because the link between the complication that, in his opinion, caused it had not been discovered (by the researcher himself) until three years after the woman's kidneys had failed. "A learned professional, very qualified," one juror said.

Yet several had reservations about him: "He seemed much more interested in research than in people," said another juror. "His testimony was sometimes irrelevant.

He'd show slides of intestinal diseases that had no bearing on the case."

"He was honest, but as the cross-examination got further and further into the details, there was only so much he could say in favor of the defendants," the jury foreman recalled.

The conflicting testimony of the expert witnesses made a vivid impression on the jury panel. "It changed my perception of medicine—it's more an art than a science," said the salesman. "That's the point the defense was trying to make. These experts couldn't agree even on simple things."

The expert witness who rated the highest with jurors was a hospital nephrologist who appeared for the plaintiffs. "He went out on a limb and testified against his colleagues, and I'm sure he got a lot of flak about that," said the motorcycle mechanic. "Though the patient had died, he still wanted to protect other patients from what happened to her."

The jurors' descriptions of the witness—"professional," "dedicated," "caring," "knowledgeable," "conscientious"—indicate the powerful effect he had on them. "His testimony was like the Bible—unshakable," said the warehouse worker.

At one point in the trial, an expert witness for the defense testified that a renal biopsy would have been too risky for the patient. The nephrologist, who had finished his testimony, returned to refute that claim, stating that he'd performed more than 300 kidney biopsies and had had only minor complications in three cases. "He didn't want to come back to court, but he did," said the steelworker. "He told us that the woman was lying there dying, and the doctors didn't do this test, which might have saved her life."

Although at least five attorneys were involved, the jury considered the trial a face-off between the plaintiff's attorney and the attorney for the internist. The physician's attorney "should have had his own television show," said one. "He was very well-dressed, forceful, and confident—all pro."

But other jurors were turned off by his demeanor. "He was just like his client, a little cocky—they were perfectly matched," the secretary said. "I remember him always playing with his gold pocket watch. I don't know why it bothered me, but it did."

Several jurors criticized the internist's attorney for repeatedly bringing up his client's credentials. "He kept referring to the doctor's membership in the American College of Physicians, but that and board certification are not the only ways to measure a doctor's competence," said the bank employee.

The jurors were also surprised by his closing argument. "He gave the impression that his client had already bought the farm, and he just wanted to keep damages to a minimum," said the warehouse worker.

There were many good words from the jury for the plaintiff's attorney. Some typical comments: "He just had all the answers." "Anything he said, he backed up with evidence." "He didn't leave a stone unturned."

"When I went into that jury room," the foreman recalled, "I wanted to give the defendants every chance. If they were liable, then justice had to be done. But if they weren't liable, I wasn't going to let anyone take them to the cleaners."

The jurors had little trouble finding the hospital liable. It had been accused, among other things, of failing to detect kidney abnormalities in an X-ray of the patient. The only question was whether the hospital or its radiologists, acting as independent contractors, should have been sued. The jurors decided the hospital was the proper defendant. "When you go into a hospital, you don't have any choice about where you get your X-rays taken," explained the steelworker. "You're putting yourself completely in the hospital's hands."

When discussion turned to the physician-defendants, a stumbling block developed. "We sent a note to the judge asking him to clarify the difference between two counts that were very similar, but he just told us to read the instructions and it would be clear," the foreman said. After a lengthy debate on that subject, the deliberations were brief.

"There was no doubt about the internist," the foreman said. They argued awhile about the surgeon, then decided that he'd been too involved in the patient's postoperative care to avoid liability.

The salesman summarized what many on the panel felt about the physician-defendants. "I wouldn't say that either of them was more or less competent than the average doctor, but there were so many errors of judgment that someone had to be at fault. There was no defense for what happened." The machinist added, "Both of them are fine men, no doubt, educated and qualified. But to put it simply, they neglected the case."

The nephrologist's testimony was critical. "He pointed out that the lady had gone unattended for kidney failure, and that led me to believe everything the doctors and the hospital had done had been wrong," asserted the welfare caseworker. The autoworker agreed. "If I saw all those tests going in one direction and didn't know why, I'd call in someone who did know. I wasn't trying to figure out why the doctors and the hospital didn't do their duty. All I know is that they didn't do it."

One or two jurors felt sorry for the surgeon. "He stayed on the case too long," said one. But they were unanimous in their feelings about the internist. "He got what he deserved," declared the secretary. "I wish we could have socked 75 percent of the damages to him, but we couldn't."

The jury spent 17 hours debating the damages. The plaintiff's attorney had asked for $4.5 million, but the jurors felt that was too high. They finally settled on $3.3 million to cover the patient's medical bills, lost earnings during her illness, and the future cost of caring for her handicapped daughter.

I asked the jurors if the trial had affected their opinions of doctors. "I'm not exactly more suspicious of doctors, but I want to know more about what they're doing to me," said the motorcycle mechanic. A 65-year-old retired sewing machine operator said: "I now ask my doctor more questions about my hypertension and arthritis medications. What are the side effects? What can go wrong? I'm not afraid to ask those questions anymore—and I feel better about my doctor now."

Several said they'd want to get second opinions on surgery in the future. "I'm supposed to have some bunions removed," said the secretary, "and I may even want a second opinion on that." The autoworker said he'd obtained a second opinion on hip surgery for his elderly aunt after doctors told her nothing could be done. "She had the operation, and she's doing fine," he said.

"There's not enough love in the medical profession today," another juror summed up. "It's a bad attitude. A human life doesn't mean that much to them. You can't say that about all doctors, of course, but too many are that way."

How Malpractice Juries Really Think

The jurors in the malpractice trial described in this chapter say many notions physicians have about lay juries are wrong. Some examples:

1. Malpractice cases are too technical for the average person to decide. Baloney! said the jurors, whose formal education ranged from eighth grade to several years of college. "By the end of that trial, we knew everything from nephrocalcinosis to hyperoxaluria," said a 28-year-old warehouse worker. "They told us we were going to get a minieducation in medicine, and we did." A motorcycle mechanic, 25, added, "We were given as much knowledge about the technical aspects of the case as most doctors have—maybe more."

The jurors credited expert witnesses on both sides with helping them understand the technical issues. "I think I could still tell you how to do a renal biopsy; it was explained so clearly to us," said a 25-year-old salesman. The jury foreman, a 29-year-old printshop supervisor, noted, "If the attorneys present the case properly, jurors can use their common sense to come to a reasonable decision."

2. Jurors presume that a bad outcome must have been the result of malpractice. "No, just because someone dies or is injured, that doesn't mean there was negligence," said a 42-year-old steelworker. A 29-year-old secretary added, "I believe some things happen that we can't do anything about, and if I were in a situation like that, I don't know if I'd necessarily sue."

3. Juries vote with their hearts, not their heads. The jurors insisted that they were not swayed by sympathy, even in this emotionally charged case.

"I wasn't looking at the emotions, even when the dead woman's invalid daughter came into the courtroom in a wheelchair," said a 46-year-old bank operations officer. "You feel compassion for the injured parties in the courtroom, but in the jury room you put that aside and deal with the facts."

The secretary admitted being moved by a tape-recorded deposition given by the patient shortly before her death, in which the woman described her numerous operations and the pain of dialysis. "It affected me, because it was eerie to hear a dead person talk, but I was influenced primarily by *what* she said. I made a point of refusing to allow myself to feel sympathy. I wanted to be fair."

4. Jurors grant generous awards because the insurance company pays. "We just followed the judge's instructions and didn't worry about who was going to pay," the salesman asserted. "Even if someone had told me the doctors' insurance would go sky-high if we made a big award, that wouldn't have made a difference."

"I knew there was such a thing as malpractice insurance," said the warehouse worker, "but I didn't know how the defendants would pay, and it never entered my mind to be concerned about that." The motorcycle mechanic added, "We knew the doctors had a lot to lose in both money and reputation."

5. Jurors make big malpractice awards to punish doctors. Money alone couldn't compensate the plaintiffs, the jurors said. One juror summed up their views: "Whether we awarded $50 or $50 million, it wouldn't have brought the patient back." Another typical reply: "We weren't trying to punish anyone, just to right a wrong, as far as possible."

INDEX

ROBERT S. BLOCKSTEIN, M.D., P.C.
MELLON PAVILION
4815 LIBERTY AVENUE
PITTSBURGH, PA. 15224

Other titles of related interest from
MEDICAL ECONOMICS BOOKS

YOUR FAMILY AND THE LAW
Jack E. Horsley, J.D., with John Carlova
ISBN 0-87489-096-9

CLINICAL ASPECTS OF MALPRACTICE
Robert S. Pollack, M.D.
ISBN 0-87489-230-9

ETHICAL OPTIONS IN MEDICINE
Gregory E. Pence, Ph.D.
ISBN 0-87489-233-3

EVALUATING ORTHOPEDIC DISABILITY: A COMMON-SENSE APPROACH
T. Rothrock Miller, M.D.
ISBN 0-87489-214-7

INSURANCE STRATEGIES FOR PHYSICIANS
Phillips Huston
ISBN 0-87489-279-1

DRUG INTERACTIONS INDEX
Fred Lerman, M.D., and Robert T. Weibert, Pharm.D.
ISBN 0-87489-266-X